D0579014

Legal Research Made Easy

Fourth Edition

Suzan D. Herskowitz and James E. Duggan
Attorneys at Law

SPHINX® PUBLISHING
AN IMPRINT OF SOURCEBOOKS, INC.®
NAPERVILLE, ILLINOIS
www.SphinxLegal.com

Fourth Edition: 2005

Published by: **Sphinx® Publishing, A Imprint of Sourcebooks, Inc.®**

Naperville Office
P.O. Box 4410
Naperville, Illinois 60567-4410
(630) 961-3900
Fax: 630-961-2168
www.sourcebooks.com
www.SphinxLegal.com

This publication is designed to provide accurate and authoritative information in regard to the subject matter covered. It is sold with the understanding that the publisher is not engaged in rendering legal, accounting, or other professional service. If legal advice or other expert assistance is required, the services of a competent professional person should be sought.

From a Declaration of Principles Jointly Adopted by a Committee of the American Bar Association and a Committee of Publishers and Associations

This product is not a substitute for legal advice.

Disclaimer required by Texas statutes.

Library of Congress Cataloging-in-Publication Data

Singer, Suzan Herskowitz, 1961-
Legal research made easy / Suzan D. Herskowitz, James E. Duggan.-- 4th ed.
p. cm.
Includes index.
ISBN 1-57248-509-4 (alk. paper)
ISBN 13 978-1-57248-509-9
1. Legal research--United States--Popular works. I. Duggan, James E., 1961- II. Title.

KF240.H47 2005
340'.072'073--dc22

2005014541

Printed and bound in the United States of America.
BG — 10 9 8 7 6 5 4 3 2 1

Contents

Using Self-Help Law Books

Before using a self-help law book, you should realize the advantages and disadvantages of doing your own legal work, and understand the challenges and diligence that this requires.

The Growing Trend

Rest assured that you will not be the first or only person handling your own legal matter. For example, in some states, more than 75% of the people in divorces and other cases represent themselves. Because of the high cost of legal services, this is a major trend and many courts are struggling to make it easier for people to represent themselves. However, some courts are not happy with people who do not use attorneys and refuse to help them in any way. For some, the attitude is, "Go to the law library and figure it out for yourself."

We write and publish self-help law books to give people an alternative to the often complicated and confusing legal books found in most law libraries. We have made the explanations of the law as simple and easy to understand as possible. Of course, unlike an attorney advising an individual client, we cannot cover every conceivable possibility.

Cost/Value Analysis

Whenever you shop for a product or service, you are faced with various levels of quality and price. In deciding what product or service to buy, you make a cost/value analysis on the basis of your willingness to pay and the quality you desire.

When buying a car, you decide whether you want transportation, comfort, status, or sex appeal. Accordingly, you decide among such choices as a Neon, a Lincoln, a Rolls Royce, or a Porsche. Before making a decision, you usually weigh the merits of each option against the cost.

When you get a headache, you can take a pain reliever (such as aspirin) or visit a medical specialist for a neurological examination. Given this choice, most people, of course, take a pain reliever, since it costs only pennies; whereas a medical examination costs hundreds of dollars and takes a lot of time. This is usually a logical choice because it is rare to need anything more than a pain reliever for a headache. But in some cases, a headache may indicate a brain tumor and failing to see a specialist right away can result in complications. Should everyone with a headache go to a specialist? Of course not, but people treating their own illnesses must realize that they are betting on the basis of their cost/value analysis of the situation. They are taking the most logical option.

The same cost/value analysis must be made when deciding to do one's own legal work. Many legal situations are very straight forward, requiring a simple form and no complicated analysis. Anyone with a little intelligence and a book of instructions can handle the matter without outside help.

But there is always the chance that complications are involved that only an attorney would notice. To simplify the law into a book like this, several legal cases often must be condensed into a single sentence or paragraph. Otherwise, the book would be several hundred pages long and too complicated for most people. However, this simplification necessarily leaves out many details and nuances that would apply to special or unusual situations. Also, there are many ways to interpret most legal questions. Your case may come before a judge who disagrees with the analysis of our authors.

Therefore, in deciding to use a self-help law book and to do your own legal work, you must realize that you are making a cost/value analysis. You have decided that the money you will save in doing it yourself outweighs the chance that your case will not turn out to your satisfaction. Most people handling their own simple legal matters never have a problem, but occasionally people find that it ended up costing them more to have an attorney straighten out the situation than it would have if they had hired an attorney in the beginning. Keep this in mind while handling your case, and be sure to consult an attorney if you feel you might need further guidance.

Local Rules

The next thing to remember is that a book which covers the law for the entire nation, or even for an entire state, cannot possibly include every procedural difference of every jurisdiction. Whenever possible, we provide the exact form needed; however, in some areas, each county, or even each judge, may require unique forms and procedures. In our state books, our forms usually cover the majority of counties in the state, or provide examples of the type of form which will be required. In our national books, our forms are sometimes even more general in nature but are designed to give a good idea of the type of form that will be needed in most locations. Nonetheless, keep in mind that your state, county, or judge may have a requirement or use a form that is not included in this book.

You should not necessarily expect to be able to get all of the information and resources you need solely from within the pages of this book. This book will serve as your guide, giving you specific information whenever possible and helping you to find out what else you will need to know. This is just like if you decided to build your own backyard deck. You might purchase a book on how to build decks. However, such a book would not include the building codes and permit requirements of every city, town, county, and township in the nation; nor would it include the lumber, nails, saws, hammers, and other materials and tools you would need to actually build the deck. You would use the book as your guide, and then do some work and research involving such matters as whether you need a permit of some kind, what type and grade of wood are available in your area, whether to use hand tools or power tools, and how to use those tools.

Before using the forms in a book like this, you should check with your court clerk to see if there are any local rules of which you should be aware, or local forms you will need to use. Often, such forms will require the same information as the forms in the book but are merely laid out differently or use slightly different language. They will sometimes require additional information.

Changes in the Law

Besides being subject to local rules and practices, the law is subject to change at any time. The courts and the legislatures of all fifty states are constantly revising the laws. It is possible that while you are reading this book, some aspect of the law is being changed.

In most cases, the change will be of minimal significance. A form will be redesigned, additional information will be required, or a waiting period will be extended. As a result, you might need to revise a form, file an extra form, or wait out a longer time period; these types of changes will not usually affect the outcome of your case. On the other hand, sometimes a major part of the law is changed, the entire law in a particular area is rewritten, or a case that was the basis of a central legal point is overruled. In such instances, your entire ability to pursue your case may be impaired.

Again, you should weigh the value of your case against the cost of an attorney and make a decision as to what you believe is in your best interest.This book is written to help Texas residents quickly and easily make their own wills without the expense or delay of hiring a lawyer. It begins with a short explanation of how a will works and what a will can and cannot do. It is designed to allow those with simple estates to quickly and inexpensively set up their affairs to distribute their property according to their wishes. It also includes an explanation of how such things as joint property, pay on death accounts, life insurance, and retirement plans will affect your planning.

Introduction

When most nonlawyers walk into a law library to do research, they are immediately awed by the vast array of books. The sheer number of them is intimidating, and the prospect of trying to do research in them is frightening. Digests? Case reporters? Looseleaf services? Statutes and codes? What are they? What are they for? Most importantly, how does one use them?

Most people reason that among all of those books, there has to be one that will yield all the information they need. These people expect that every answer to every question they have on a particular topic will be in one volume—a nice, neat little package. Unfortunately, research in a law library is not that nice or neat. It tends to take time, and rarely will people find all the information they are seeking in one place.

Why would you do your own legal research? Perhaps your lawyer said you would save money if you helped with research. Perhaps you do not want to hire a lawyer. Perhaps you are not even sure you need a lawyer. One thing is certain, however—if you need legal information about a particular problem, you must go to a law library.

Now you are standing inside that law library, looking at all of those books, and you are afraid you will never find what you are looking for.

This guide is designed to take some of that fear out of legal research. In it, you will find an explanation of how to do legal research, as well as descriptions of the main sources of information necessary for effective legal research. There are tables and examples of each source throughout, which will put it all in perspective. The appendix gives an example of a legal problem and how you would go about conducting research on it. This will help you *put it all together* and see how the various sources interrelate.

While this book is designed specifically for those who are not familiar with the legal system or legal research, it can be an effective tool or refresher for anyone in the profession, whether that person is a lawyer, law student, paralegal, or legal secretary.

Where to Start

chapter 1

A law library is a must for effective legal research. It is the only place you can go for *one-stop shopping* when you have a legal problem. However, you may not be familiar with the culture of a law library. This chapter teaches you where to find a library and what to expect once you get there. This chapter also helps you get your feet wet by explaining how to begin the process of solving your problem.

WHERE TO FIND LAW LIBRARIES

Generally, there are two locations where a law library can be found. The first is at the county courthouse and the second is on a law school campus.

County Law Libraries

Most county governments fund a law library. Depending on the size of the county, the library collection can be small or quite extensive. It may cover a large area, or simply consist of a few shelves in an office or conference room adjacent to the judge's chambers. In almost all circumstances, the library is located within the main courthouse in the county seat. Since these libraries are publicly owned and supported by tax dollars, they are generally open to the public during regular courthouse hours. Some may be open on select evenings and weekends, but you cannot depend on that. They usually have a law *librarian* available to offer assistance, but that assistance may be limited due to staffing and time constraints. In smaller counties, the judge's secretary or law clerk may double as the librarian.

You will usually find the phone number for the *county law library* in the white or blue pages of your local phone directory in the county government section. If it is not listed under a separate heading of "library" or "law library," you may find it listed as a subheading under "courthouse." If all else fails, call the county's main information number for assistance.

Law School Libraries

Access to a *law school library* may depend on whether the law school is a public or private institution. In general, a public university law school library will have open public access. Private university law library access may be open, limited, or closed, depending upon the policy of the law library.

If you have a law school in your area, use your local white pages telephone directory to look up the university. Then, find the subheading for the law school. The library's main number is generally listed under "law library."

The person at the library's information or circulation desk will be able to give you information about public access and hours. All law school libraries have restricted hours during exams and school breaks, so be sure to call if it is the end of the fall or spring semester, during the summer, or close to a holiday. Otherwise, you may get to the library and find it restricted to the public or closed.

The information desk will also be able to tell you what type of librarian assistance is available. Do not be surprised if it is limited, even for public universities, since the library's main objective is to serve the students and faculty of the institution.

NOTE: *Alaska does not currently have a university that offers a law program.*

Law Schools by State

Alabama

Samford University (Cumberland)
800 Lakeshore Drive
Birmingham, AL 35229
http://cumberland.samford.edu
Private

University of Alabama
Box 870382
Tuscaloosa, AL 35487
www.law.ua.edu
Public

Arizona

Arizona State University
Box 877906
Tempe, AZ 85287-7906
www.law.asu.edu
Public

University of Arizona (Rogers)
James E. Rogers College of Law
P.O. Box 210176
Tucson, AZ 85721-0176
www.law.arizona.edu
Public

Arkansas

University of Arkansas—Fayetteville
School of Law
107 Waterman Hall
Fayetteville, AR 72701
http://law.uark.edu
Public

University of Arkansas—Little Rock (Bowen)
1201 McMath Avenue
Little Rock, AR 72202-5142
www.law.ualr.edu
Public

California

California Western School of Law
225 Cedar Street
San Diego, CA 92101-3090
www.cwsl.edu
Private

Chapman University
1 University Drive
Orange, CA 92866
www.chapman.edu/law
Private

Golden Gate University
536 Mission Street
San Francisco, CA 94105
www.ggu.edu/law
Private

Loyola Law School
919 Albany Street
Los Angeles, CA 90015-1211
www.lls.edu
Private

Pepperdine University
24255 Pacific Coast Highway
Malibu, CA 90263
http://law.pepperdine.edu
Private

Santa Clara University
500 El Camino Real
Santa Clara, CA 95053-0421
www.scu.edu/law
Private

Southwestern University School of Law
675 South Westmoreland Avenue
Los Angeles, CA 90005-3992
www.swlaw.edu
Private

Stanford University
Crown Quadrangle
559 Nathan Abbott Way
Stanford, CA 94305-8610
www.law.stanford.edu
Private

Thomas Jefferson School of Law
2121 San Diego Avenue
San Diego, CA 92110
www.tjsl.edu
Private

University of California (Hastings)
200 McAllister Street
San Francisco, CA 94102
www.uchastings.edu
Public

University of California—Berkeley
School of Law
(Boalt Hall)
Berkeley, CA 94720-7200
www.law.berkeley.edu
Public

University of California—Davis
School of Law
400 Mrak Hall Drive
Davis, CA 95616-5201
www.law.ucdavis.edu
Public

University of California—Los Angeles
71 Dodd Hall
P.O. Box 951445
Los Angeles, CA 90095-1445
www.law.ucla.edu
Public

University of San Diego
5998 Alcala Park
San Diego, CA 92110-2492
www.sandiego.edu/usdlaw
Private

University of San Francisco
2130 Fulton Street
San Francisco, CA 94117-1080
www.law.usfca.edu
Private

University of Southern California
Law School
Los Angeles, CA 90089-0071
www.usc.edu/law
Private

University of the Pacific (McGeorge)
3200 Fifth Avenue
Sacramento, CA 95817
www.mcgeorge.edu
Private

Western State University
1111 North State College Boulevard
Fullerton, CA 92831
www.wsulaw.edu
Private

Whittier Law School
3333 Harbor Boulevard
Costa Mesa, CA 92626-1501
www.law.whittier.edu
Private

Colorado

University of Colorado—Boulder
Box 403
Boulder, CO 80309-0403
www.colorado.edu/law
Public

University of Denver
2255 East Evans Avenue
Denver, CO 80208
www.law.du.edu
Private

Connecticut

Quinnipiac University
275 Mount Carmel Avenue
Hamden, CT 06518
http://law.quinnipiac.edu
Private

University of Connecticut
55 Elizabeth Street
Hartford, CT 06105-2296
www.law.uconn.edu
Public

Yale University
P.O. Box 208215
New Haven, CT 06520-8215
www.law.yale.edu
Private

Delaware

Widener University
P.O. Box 7474
Wilmington, DE 19803-0474
www.law.widener.edu
Private

District of Columbia

American University (Washington)
4801 Massachusetts Avenue N.W.
Washington, DC 20016-8192
www.wcl.american.edu
Private

Catholic University of America
School of Law
Washington, DC 20064
www.law.edu
Private

George Washington University
2000 H Street N.W.
Washington, DC 20052
www.law.gwu.edu
Private

Georgetown University
600 New Jersey Avenue N.W.
Washington, DC 20001
www.law.georgetown.edu
Private

Howard University
2900 Van Ness Street N.W.
Washington, DC 20008
www.law.howard.edu
Private

University of the District of Columbia
4250 Connecticut Avenue, N.W.
Building 48
Washington, DC 20008
www.law.udc.edu
Public

Florida

Barry University
6441 East Colonial Drive
Orlando, FL 32807
www.barry.edu/law
Private

Florida Coastal School of Law
7555 Beach Boulevard
Jacksonville, FL 32216
www.fcsl.edu
Private

Florida State University
425 West Jefferson Street
Tallahassee, FL 32306-1601
www.law.fsu.edu
Public

Nova Southeastern University
3305 College Avenue
Fort Lauderdale, FL 33314-7721
www.nsulaw.nova.edu
Private

St. Thomas University
16400 N.W. 32nd Avenue
Miami, FL 33054
www.stu.edu
Private

Stetson University
1401 61st Street South
Gulfport, FL 33707
www.law.stetson.edu
Private

University of Florida (Levin)
Levin College of Law
P.O. Box 117620
Gainesville, FL 32611-7620
www.law.ufl.edu
Public

University of Miami
P.O. Box 248087
Coral Gables, FL 33124-8087
www.law.miami.edu
Private

Georgia

Emory University
1301 Clifton Road
Atlanta, GA 30322-2770
www.law.emory.edu
Private

Georgia State University
P.O. Box 4049
Atlanta, GA 30302-4049
http://law.gsu.edu
Public

Mercer University
1021 Georgia Avenue
Macon, GA 31207-0001
www.law.mercer.edu
Private

University of Georgia
Herty Drive
Athens, GA 30602
www.lawsch.uga.edu
Public

Hawaii

University of Hawaii
2515 Dole Street
Honolulu, HI 96822
www.hawaii.edu/law
Public

Idaho

University of Idaho
College of Law
P.O. Box 442321
Moscow, ID 83844-2321
www.law.uidaho.edu
Public

Illinois

DePaul University
25 East Jackson Boulevard
Chicago, IL 60604
www.law.depaul.edu
Private

Illinois Institute of Technology (Chicago-Kent)
565 West Adams Street
Chicago, IL 60661-3691
www.kentlaw.edu
Private

John Marshall Law School
315 South Plymouth Court
Chicago, IL 60604
www.jmls.edu
Private

Loyola University Chicago
1 East Pearson Street
Chicago, IL 60611
www.luc.edu/schools/law
Private

Northern Illinois University
College of Law
DeKalb, IL 60115
www.niu.edu/col
Public

Northwestern University
357 East Chicago Avenue
Chicago, IL 60611
www.law.northwestern.edu
Private

Southern Illinois University—Carbondale
Lesar Law Building
Carbondale, IL 62901-6804
www.law.siu.edu
Public

University of Chicago
1111 East 60th Street
Chicago, IL 60637
www.law.uchicago.edu
Private

University of Illinois—Urbana-Champaign
504 East Pennsylvania Avenue
Champaign, IL 61820
www.law.uiuc.edu
Public

Indiana

Indiana University—Bloomington
School of Law
211 South Indiana Avenue
Bloomington, IN 47405-1001
www.law.indiana.edu
Public

Indiana University—Indianapolis
530 West New York Street
Indianapolis, IN 46202-3225
www.indylaw.indiana.edu
Public

University of Notre Dame
Notre Dame Law School
P.O. Box R
Notre Dame, IN 46556-0780
www.lawadmissions.nd.edu
Private

Valparaiso University
Wesemann Hall
Valparaiso, IN 46383
www.valpo.edu/law
Private

Iowa

Drake University
2507 University Avenue
Des Moines, IA 50311
www.law.drake.edu
Private

University of Iowa
276 Boyd Law Building
Iowa City, IA 52242
www.uiowa.edu/~lawcoll
Public

Kansas

University of Kansas
Green Hall
1535 West 15th Street
Lawrence, KS 66045-7577
www.law.ku.edu
Public

Washburn University
1700 College
Topeka, KS 66621
http://washburnlaw.edu
Public

Kentucky

Northern Kentucky University (Chase)
Nunn Hall
Highland Heights, KY 41099-6031
www.nku.edu/~chase
Public

University of Kentucky
209 Law Building
Lexington, KY 40506-0048
www.uky.edu/law
Public

University of Louisville (Brandeis)
School of Law
Louisville, KY 40292
www.louisville.edu/brandeislaw
Public

Louisiana

Louisiana State University—Baton Rouge
400 Paul M. Hebert Law Center
Baton Rouge, LA 70803
www.law.lsu.edu
Public

Loyola University—New Orleans
7214 St. Charles Avenue
New Orleans, LA 70118
http://law.loyno.edu
Private

Southern University
P.O. Box 9294
Baton Rouge, LA 70813
www.sus.edu/sulc
Public

Tulane University
6329 Freret Street
John Giffen Weinmann Hall
New Orleans, LA 70118-6231
www.law.tulane.edu
Private

Maine

University of Maine
246 Deering Avenue
Portland, ME 04102
www.mainelaw.maine.edu
Public

Maryland

University of Baltimore
1420 North Charles Street
Baltimore, MD 21201-5779
www.law.ubalt.edu
Public

University of Maryland
500 West Baltimore Street
Baltimore, MD 21201-1786
www.law.umaryland.edu
Public

Massachusetts

Boston College
885 Centre Street
Newton, MA 02459-1154
www.bc.edu/lawschool
Private

Boston University
765 Commonwealth Avenue
Boston, MA 02215
www.bu.edu/law
Private

Harvard University
Harvard Law School
Cambridge, MA 02138
www.law.harvard.edu
Private

New England School of Law
154 Stuart Street
Boston, MA 02116
www.nesl.edu
Private

Northeastern University
400 Huntington Avenue
Boston, MA 02115
www.slaw.neu.edu
Private

Suffolk University
120 Tremont Street
Boston, MA 02108
www.law.suffolk.edu
Private

Western New England College
1215 Wilbraham Road
Springfield, MA 01119-2684
www.law.wnec.edu
Private

Michigan

Ave Maria School of Law
3475 Plymouth Road
Ann Arbor, MI 48105-2550
www.avemarialaw.edu
Private

Michigan State University—DCL College of Law
368 Law College Building
East Lansing, MI 48824-1300
www.law.msu.edu
Private

Thomas M. Cooley Law School
300 South Capitol Avenue
P.O. Box 13038
Lansing, MI 48901
www.cooley.edu
Private

University of Detroit Mercy
651 East Jefferson Avenue
Detroit, MI 48226
www.law.udmercy.edu
Private

University of Michigan—Ann Arbor
625 South State Street
Ann Arbor, MI 48109
www.law.umich.edu
Public

Wayne State University
471 West Palmer Street
Detroit, MI 48202
www.law.wayne.edu
Public

Minnesota

Hamline University
1536 Hewitt Avenue
St. Paul, MN 55104-1284
www.hamline.edu/law
Private

University of Minnesota—Twin Cities
229 19th Avenue S
Minneapolis, MN 55455
www.law.umn.edu
Public

William Mitchell College of Law
875 Summit Avenue
St. Paul, MN 55105-3076
www.wmitchell.edu
Private

Mississippi

Mississippi College
151 East Griffith Street
Jackson, MS 39201
www.law.mc.edu
Private

University of Mississippi
Law Center
P.O. Box 1848
University, MS 38677
www.olemiss.edu/depts/law_school
Public

Missouri

St. Louis University
3700 Lindell Boulevard
St. Louis, MO 63108
http://law.slu.edu
Private

University of Missouri—Columbia
203 Hulston Hall
Columbia, MO 65211-4300
www.law.missouri.edu
Public

University of Missouri—Kansas City
5100 Rockhill Road
Kansas City, MO 64110
www.law.umkc.edu
Public

Washington University in St. Louis
1 Brookings Drive
Box 1120
St. Louis, MO 63130
www.law.wustl.edu
Private

Montana

University of Montana
School of Law
Missoula, MT 59812
www.umt.edu/law
Public

Nebraska

Creighton University
2500 California Plaza
Omaha, NE 68178
http://culaw2.creighton.edu
Private

University of Nebraska—Lincoln
College of Law
P.O. Box 830902
Lincoln, NE 68583-0902
http://law.unl.edu
Public

Nevada

University of Nevada—Las Vegas (William S. Boyd)
4505 Maryland Parkway
Box 451003
Las Vegas, NV 89154-1003
www.law.unlv.edu
Public

New Hampshire

Franklin Pierce Law Center
Two White Street
Concord, NH 03301
www.piercelaw.edu
Private

New Jersey

Rutgers State University—Camden
217 North Fifth Street
Camden, NJ 08102-1203
www-camlaw.rutgers.edu
Public

Rutgers State University—Newark
Rutgers Law School
123 Washington Street
Newark, NJ 7102
http://law.newark.rutgers.edu
Public

Seton Hall University
1 Newark Center
Newark, NJ 07102-5210
http://law.shu.edu
Private

New Mexico

University of New Mexico
1117 Stanford Drive N.E.
Albuquerque, NM 87131-1431
http://lawschool.unm.edu
Public

New York

Albany Law School-Union University
80 New Scotland Avenue
Albany, NY 12208-3494
www.als.edu
Private

Brooklyn Law School
250 Joralemon Street
Brooklyn, NY 11201
www.brooklaw.edu
Private

Cardozo-Yeshiva University
55 Fifth Avenue
10th Floor
New York, NY 10003
www.cardozo.yu.edu
Private

Columbia University
435 West 116th Street
New York, NY 10027
www.law.columbia.edu
Private

Cornell University
Myron Taylor Hall
Ithaca, NY 14853-4901
www.lawschool.cornell.edu
Private

CUNY—Queens College
65-21 Main Street
Flushing, NY 11367
www.law.cuny.edu
Public

Fordham University
140 W. 62nd Street
New York, NY 10023
http://law.fordham.edu/index.htm
Private

Hofstra University
121 Hofstra University
Hempstead, NY 11549
www.hofstra.edu/law
Private

New York Law School
57 Worth Street
New York, NY 10013-2960
www.nyls.edu
Private

New York University
40 Washington Square S
New York, NY 10012
www.law.nyu.edu
Private

Pace University
78 North Broadway
White Plains, NY 10603
www.law.pace.edu
Private

St. John's University
8000 Utopia Parkway
Jamaica, NY 11439
www.law.stjohns.edu
Private

Syracuse University
College of Law
Syracuse, NY 13244-1030
www.law.syr.edu
Private

Touro College (Jacob D. Fuchsberg)
300 Nassau Road
Huntington, NY 11743
www.tourolaw.edu
Private

University at Buffalo—SUNY
John Lord O'Brian Hall
Buffalo, NY 14260
www.law.buffalo.edu
Public

North Carolina

Campbell University
Box 158
Buies Creek, NC 27506
http://law.campbell.edu
Private

Duke University
Towerview and Science Drive
Box 90362
Durham, NC 27708-0362
www.law.duke.edu
Private

North Carolina Central University
1512 South Alston Avenue
Durham, NC 27707
www.acc.nccu.edu/law
Public

University of North Carolina—Chapel Hill
Van Hecke-Wettach Hall
CB No. 3380
Chapel Hill, NC 27599-3380
www.law.unc.edu
Public

Wake Forest University
Reynolds Station
P.O. Box 7206
Winston-Salem, NC 27109
www.law.wfu.edu
Private

North Dakota

University of North Dakota
P.O. Box 9003
Grand Forks, ND 58202
www.law.und.nodak.edu
Public

Ohio

Capital University
303 East Broad Street
Columbus, OH 43215-3200
www.law.capital.edu
Private

Case Western Reserve University
11075 East Boulevard
Cleveland, OH 44106-7148
www.law.case.edu
Private

Cleveland State University (Marshall)
2121 Euclid Avenue
LB 138
Cleveland, OH 44115-2214
www.law.csuohio.edu
Public

Ohio Northern University
525 South Main Street
Ada, OH 45810-1599
www.law.onu.edu
Private

Ohio State University (Moritz)
55 West 12th Avenue
Columbus, OH 43210
www.osu.edu/units/law
Public

Ohio University of Akron
C. Blake McDowell Law Center
Akron, OH 44325-2901
www.uakron.edu/law
Public

University of Cincinnati
P.O. Box 210040
Cincinnati, OH 45221-0040
www.law.uc.edu
Public

University of Dayton
300 College Park
Dayton, OH 45469-2772
www.law.udayton.edu
Private

University of Toledo
2801 West Bancroft
Toledo, OH 43606
www.utlaw.edu
Public

Oklahoma

Oklahoma City University
2501 North Blackwelder
Oklahoma City, OK 73106-1493
www.okcu.edu/law
Private

University of Oklahoma
300 Timberdell Road
Norman, OK 73019-5081
www.law.ou.edu
Public

University of Tulsa
3120 East Fourth Place
Tulsa, OK 74104
www.law.utulsa.edu
Private

Oregon

Lewis and Clark College (Northwestern)
10015 S.W. Terwilliger Boulevard
Portland, OR 97219
http://law.lclark.edu
Private

University of Oregon
1221 University of Oregon
Eugene, OR 97403-1221
www.law.uoregon.edu
Public

Willamette University
245 Winter Street S.E.
Salem, OR 97301-3922
www.willamette.edu/wucl
Private

Pennsylvania

Duquesne University
600 Forbes Avenue
Pittsburgh, PA 15282
www.duq.edu/law
Private

Penn State University (Dickinson School of Law)
150 South College Street
Carlisle, PA 17013-2899
www.dsl.psu.edu
Private

Temple University (Beasley)
1719 North Broad Street
Philadelphia, PA 19122
www.temple.edu/lawschool
Public

University of Pennsylvania
3400 Chestnut Street
Philadelphia, PA 19104-6204
www.law.upenn.edu
Private

University of Pittsburgh
3900 Forbes Avenue
Pittsburgh, PA 15260
www.law.pitt.edu
Public

Villanova University
299 North Spring Mill Road
Villanova, PA 19085
www.law.villanova.edu
Private

Puerto Rico

Catholic University
2250 Avenida Las Americas
Suite 584
Ponce, PR 00717-0777
www.pucpr.edu
Private

Inter-American University
P.O. Box 70351
San Juan, PR 00936-8351
www.metro.inter.edu
Private

University of Puerto Rico
P.O. Box 23303 Estacion Universidad
Rio Piedras, PR 00931-3302
www.upr.edu
Public

Rhode Island

Roger Williams University
10 Metacom Avenue
Bristol, RI 02809-5171
http://law.rwu.edu
Private

South Carolina

University of South Carolina
701 South Main Street
Columbia, SC 29208
www.law.sc.edu
Public

South Dakota

University of South Dakota
414 East Clark Street
Vermillion, SD 57069-2390
www.usd.edu/law
Public

Tennessee

University of Memphis
207 Humphreys Law School
Memphis, TN 38152-3140
www.law.memphis.edu
Public

University of Tennessee—Knoxville
1505 West Cumberland Avenue
Knoxville, TN 37996-1810
www.law.utk.edu
Public

Vanderbilt University
131 21st Avenue S
Nashville, TN 37203
www.vanderbilt.edu/law
Private

Texas

Baylor University
1114 South University Parks Drive
Waco, TX 76706
http://law.baylor.edu
Private

South Texas College of Law
1303 San Jacinto Street
Houston, TX 77002-7000
www.stcl.edu
Private

Southern Methodist University
P.O. Box 750116
Dallas, TX 75275-0116
www.law.smu.edu
Private

St. Mary's University
One Camino Santa Maria
San Antonio, TX 78228-8602
http://law.stmarytx.edu
Private

Texas Southern University (Thurgood Marshall)
3100 Cleburne Street
Houston, TX 77004
www.tsulaw.edu
Public

Texas Tech University
1802 Hartford Avenue
Lubbock, TX 79409
www.law.ttu.edu
Public

Texas Wesleyan University
1515 Commerce Street
Fort Worth, TX 76102
www.law.txwes.edu
Private

University of Houston
100 Law Center
Houston, TX 77204-6060
www.law.uh.edu
Public

University of Texas—Austin
727 East Dean Keeton Street
Austin, TX 78705-3299
www.utexas.edu/law
Public

Utah

Brigham Young University (J. Reuben Clark)
340 JRCB
Provo, UT 84602
www.law.byu.edu
Private

University of Utah (S.J. Quinney)
332 South 1400 E
Room 101
Salt Lake City, UT 84112
www.law.utah.edu
Public

Vermont

Vermont Law School
Chelsea Street
South Royalton, VT 05068-0096
www.vermontlaw.edu
Private

Virginia

Appalachian School of Law
P.O. Box 2825
Grundy, VA 24614-2825
www.asl.edu
Private

College of William and Mary
P.O. Box 8795
Williamsburg, VA 23187-8795
www.wm.edu/law
Public

George Mason University
3301 North Fairfax Drive
Arlington, VA 22201-4426
www.law.gmu.edu
Public

Regent University
1000 Regent University Drive
Virginia Beach, VA 23464-9880
www.regent.edu/law/admissions
Private

University of Richmond
T.C. Williams School of Law
Richmond, VA 23173
http://law.richmond.edu
Private

University of Virginia
580 Massie Road
Charlottesville, VA 22903-1789
www.law.virginia.edu
Public

Washington and Lee University
Sydney Lewis Hall
Lexington, VA 24450-0303
http://law.wlu.edu/admissions
Private

Washington

Gonzaga University
P.O. Box 3528
Spokane, WA 99220-3528
http://law.gonzaga.edu
Private

Seattle University
900 Broadway
Seattle, WA 98122-4340
www.law.seattleu.edu
Private

University of Washington
Campus Box 353020
Seattle, WA 98195-3020
www.law.washington.edu
Public

West Virginia

West Virginia University
P.O. Box 6130
Morgantown, WV 26506-6130
www.wvu.edu/~law
Public

Wisconsin

Marquette University
Sensenbrenner Hall
P.O. Box 1881
Milwaukee, WI 53201-1881
http://law.marquette.edu
Private

University of Wisconsin—Madison
975 Bascom Mall
Madison, WI 53706-1399
www.law.wisc.edu
Public

Wyoming

University of Wyoming
College of Law
Department 3035
1000 East University Avenue
Laramie, WY 82071
www.uwyo.edu/law
Public

What to Bring with You—Supplies and Money

There are a few items you will find necessary at the library, and you should not expect the library to supply them. One is an ample supply of paper. Scraps of paper will not suffice, because you will be taking lots of notes. Also bring a supply of pens or sharpened pencils.

Legal research usually requires the use of a copy machine. When you are reading a case, you will want to make notes and highlight or underline portions of it. You could take down the portions by hand, but after a while, you will probably find it tedious and time-consuming. Most law libraries have copy machines, or at least offer library users access to one somewhere in the building. When you call the information desk for the hours of operation, make sure you inquire about the cost of making copies. Also ask if the library makes change, because some do not. It is best to know in advance.

Most libraries—county and law school—have what are called *copy cards*. These are plastic cards about the size of a credit card with a magnetic strip on the back. The following are some tips about copy cards and making copies.

- You pay a set price for the card, say $5.00, and you will receive a set number of copies, say sixty copies.
- When you insert the card into a reader, the card will be debited automatically each time you make a copy.

- Usually, there is a discount on the price per copy if you purchase a copy card.
- Exact change for the price of the card will probably be required, unless the library will make change for you.
- If you must purchase the card from a machine, make sure your bills are not rumpled or the machine may reject them.
- Be aware that unless there is a problem with the copy machine, the library may not reimburse you for copies made in error.
- Always check the machine's settings before you press the copy button.

YOUR LEGAL PROBLEM

Before you pick up your first law book, you must decide what your goals are. When brainstorming about your problem, your focus—and therefore your chances of finding the right information—will improve. The following is a guide for determining your goals.

1. Formulate a clear idea of what information you need.

Are you looking for information about your legal rights; for example, at your job or in a dispute with the city? Do you want to perform a specific procedure, such as filing a divorce or registering a trademark? If you want to perform a procedure, you will need a different type of book than if you want to know your rights in a dispute.

If you want to register a trademark, for example, there will be books that explain the process step-by-step. However, if you want to know if you can sue your employer for discrimination, you will have to read several statutes and many courts' decisions to see if your situation fits any of them. If you want to file for divorce, you may be able to use a simple procedure book, but if there is something unusual about your case, you may want to do further research into other court cases.

Also, decide if you are looking for an answer to a specific question (such as "Can I stop paying alimony if my ex-wife moves in with her boyfriend?"), or for more general information about an area of the law (such as "How do I go about getting a divorce?").

2. Think of all possible words and phrases that describe your research topic.

If you are trying to find information about child support, for example, you would think of words such as "child," "minor," "infant," "child support," "aid," "maintenance," etc. Write down all of the words you can think of and add them to the list as more come to mind. A thesaurus may be helpful. Ask the librarian for a copy of *Roget's* as well as a legal thesaurus. You may also want to consult a law dictionary. Ask for a copy of *Black's Law Dictionary* or *Ballentine's Law Dictionary*. A law dictionary will define legal terms that a regular dictionary will not. However, a regular dictionary, such as *Webster's* or *American Heritage,* may be helpful as well.

Lastly, you may want to consult a set of books published by West Publishing Company called *Words and Phrases*. This set consists of 107 volumes of *headnote abstracts,* which will provide you with definitions of words and phrases that are legally meaningful. In brief, a *headnote* is a short summary of a legal rule of fact in a case. (See Chapter 4 for discussions about headnotes and abstracts.) Using this set will not only yield synonyms, but will be helpful when you are unsure about the legal meaning of a word or phrase.

3. Decide whether your case involves federal law, state law, or both.

Each state and the federal government have their own sets of laws. Some cases, such as divorce, are only covered by state law, and others, such as copyright, are only covered by federal law. But some matters, such as discrimination, may be covered by both state and federal laws. In your preliminary research, you must determine which state laws are applicable to your problem and whether federal law applies.

How do you know what type of law you should research? Ask yourself what your problem involves. If your problem concerns the Internal

Revenue Service, for example, you would be interested in federal law. If your problem is associated with state taxation of income or obtaining a divorce, you would be interested in state law. The initial research you do will point you toward statutes or court cases. Note whether these are state or federal.

If you are researching state law, be sure you have the right state. Do not assume that the law in one state is the same as the law in another. Often, the laws in each state are very different from each other. (Also, federal law, if it applies, may be very different from state law.) If you think your problem may be dependent on another state's laws or more than one state's laws, you must research each state independently.

4. Decide whether you are dealing with civil or criminal law.

Sometimes this is confusing to people who are not involved daily in the legal process. How do you know if something is civil or criminal? Usually, it depends upon the party entitled to bring the lawsuit.

In general, unless there is a specific statute with criminal penalties attached to it, the matter will not involve criminal law. For example, if a person accidentally drives into the side of your house, or owes you rent and does not pay you, there will probably not be a crime involved.

If there is a crime involved and you are the victim, you will not be able to bring the criminal suit yourself. The government brings the suit not just on your behalf, but on behalf of *the people*, or all of the citizens of the state. The idea is that the peace of the community was breached by the alleged acts of the defendant, so the government, as the protector of the community and its people, deals with the problem. This concept originated with English Common Law, on which the laws in the United States are based. Anyone who breached the King's peace was guilty of a crime, and the King, through his officials, prosecuted.

However, you should not assume that if the government is a party to a lawsuit, the action must be criminal. The government can bring a civil action as well. For example, if the county wants to widen a street and needs part of your front yard, the county brings a condemnation suit using its power of eminent domain. This means the county can take your property and pay you for it. This is not a criminal action because you are not being *prosecuted* for a crime. It is only a civil action. A civil action is one not involving criminal acts, and is often brought to correct what is perceived as an injury or wrong against the person bringing the lawsuit.

In many criminal cases, the victim also has the right to bring a civil lawsuit for *compensation*, or money damages. For example, if a member of your family is murdered or injured, or if your property is criminally damaged or stolen, you can file a civil suit for damages. This suit is not part of the criminal prosecution and the state does not help you with your suit.

If you are accused of a crime, you can be subject to both prosecution by the state and a civil suit by the victim. In such a situation, you will need to know both the civil and criminal laws related to the matter.

Typically, a law book may cover one subject, or may include multiple subjects in its coverage. In addition, you may be using case law digests or other indexes that cover multiple areas of the law. To help you determine what subject your case or issue may be indexed under, look at the following selective descriptions of law subject categories.

Generally Civil

- *Administrative Law*: typically deals with rules and regulations (and interpretations) by governmental agencies and entities.

- *Agency and Partnership*: covers relationships created between agents and their principals (generally in a business or employment context), as well as business partnership and organization rules.

- *Bankruptcy*: covers personal and business debt relief and reorganization.

- *Civil Procedure*: rules covering civil trials, conduct by attorneys and parties, evidence, and appeals.

- *Commercial Law* (includes Banking, Business Law, and Commercial Paper): covers business transactions and other commercial enterprises. It also deals with actions under the Uniform Commercial Code.

- *Conflict of Laws*: covers the determination of which laws apply when multiple jurisdictions or courts are involved.

- *Constitutional Law*: covers the interpretation of the U.S. Constitution, including rights and duties of individuals and the branches of government.

- *Consumer Law*: covers purchases, contracts, and agreements between businesses and consumers, such as automobile sales, service contracts, and consumer financing.

- *Contracts* (includes Sales and Leasing): promises and duties between parties that are enforceable in law.

- *Corporations* (includes Business Law): state laws covering legal entities that have incorporated to do business or conduct other activities.

- *Estate and Gift Taxation*: covers taxation of property held by individuals at death, as well as certain gifts made to avoid tax liability.

- *Evidence*: rules about what may be used to prove something at trial.

- *Family Law* (includes Adoption, Custody, Divorce, and Marriage): covers aspects of personal relationships and obligations.

- *Federal Courts*: covers procedures and rules of the U.S. Federal Court system.

- *Intellectual Property* (includes Copyrights, Patents, and Trademarks): rights applying to inventions, writings, discoveries, and other creative works.

- *International Law* (includes Treaties and other International Agreements): rules governing relationships between nations.

- *Labor Law* (includes Employment Law and Employment Discrimination): covers relationships between employers and employees.

- *Landlord/Tenant Law*: covers the rental of commercial and residential property.

- *Professional Responsibility* (includes Legal Ethics): rules governing lawyers, judges, and other professions.

- *Property* (includes Real Estate Law): covers rights of use and disposition of things, objects, and land.

- *Remedies*: covers enforcement of court judgments, damages, and court orders.

- *Secured Transactions*: covers loan agreements secured by property or other collateral, such as mortgages and installment sales agreements.

- *Torts* (includes Negligence and Intentional Acts, and Products Liability): covers wrongs committed against a person or entity that may result in *relief* (damages or other remedies).

- *Wills, Trusts, and Estates* (includes Probate): laws determining property disposition at death and interpretation of wills.

- *Workers' Compensation*: covers rules specifying payment for injuries and disabilities occurring at the workplace.

Generally Criminal

- *Criminal Law* (includes elements of specific crimes, persons responsible, and specific penalties): laws covering the governmental prosecution of a person for criminal acts.

- *Criminal Procedure* (includes criminal trial procedures, evidence, and appeals): rules covering the process for enforcement of criminal laws.

Civil and Criminal

- *Antitrust Law*: covers business monopolies and trusts, price fixing agreements, and other restraints on trade.

- *Foreign Law*: covers laws of non-U.S. nations, countries, and localities.

- *Income Tax*: covers laws and regulations over the assessment and collection of income tax, plus penalties for nonpayment.

- *Securities Regulation*: laws dealing with investment, stocks, bonds, and other forms of securities.

Once you have completed these four steps, you can go to the books themselves and actively research your topic. If you have difficulty completing these steps, however, you will want to consult a legal encyclopedia. (see page 24.)

SUBSTANTIVE AND PROCEDURAL LAW

Most legal matters involve both *substantive* and *procedural* law. Substantive law is the law that determines whether or not something can be done, or what your *legal rights* are in a matter. For example, in a divorce, the substantive law would tell you if you can get a divorce and what the terms of the divorce can be. Procedural law is the law that determines which procedure you must use to obtain what you want. In a divorce, it tells you which papers you must file and what they must include.

Regardless of your problem or question, the best place to start is usually with a practice manual (or self-help law book), if you can find one. If not, you could start with a legal encyclopedia.

LOOKING UP PROCEDURES

If your goal is to complete a legal procedure (such as filing an adoption, registering a patent, or getting your security deposit back from a landlord), there may be simple explanations of these procedures available to you.

Law Books for Consumers

In recent years there have been many books published explaining legal procedures in simple language. Many of these are available at law libraries, public libraries, and bookstores. These include a simplified explanation of the law and often the forms needed to complete the procedure. They are usually thorough enough if your case is simple. To help you find specific law book titles, consult the following list of selected legal publishers.

For the Attorney:

Publisher	Website
Aspen Publishers, Inc.	www.aspenpublishers.com
Bureau of National Affairs (BNA)	www.bna.com
Carolina Academic Press	www.cap-press.com
CCH Incorporated	www.cch.com
Harrison Company (A Thomson Company)	http://west.thomson.com/promotions/harrison.asp
Kluwer Law International (Aspen Publishers)	www.kli.com
Knowles Publishing, Inc.	www.knowlespublishing.com
LegalWorks (A Thomson Company)	www.legalwks.com
LexisNexis	http://bookstore.lexis.com/bookstore/catalog
LRP Publications	www.lrp.com
Oceana Publications	www.oceanalaw.com
Pike & Fischer (A BNA Company)	www.pf.com
RIA (A Thomson Company)	http://ria.thomson.com/default.asp
West (A Thomson Company)	http://west.thomson.com/store/default.asp

For the Consumer:

Publisher	Website
Barron's Educational Series	http://barronseduc.com/business---finance-law.html
Dearborn Trade Publishing	www.dearborn.com/trade
John Wiley & Sons, Inc.	www.wiley.com
Jones McClure Publishing	www.jonesmcclure.com
Nolo Press	www.nolo.com
Nova Publishing	www.novapublishing.com
Sphinx Publishing	www.sphinxlegal.com

Practice Manuals for Lawyers

For most states, there are practice manuals explaining how to practice law to lawyers. Some of these books are published by private companies and others are published by the continuing legal education department of the state bar associations. Many law libraries carry these books. They can be your most useful tool in completing a legal procedure, especially when matters are more complicated than those covered by consumer legal books. These types of books are described in Chapter 2 of this book.

Statutes, Rules, and Regulations

For many procedures, the legal requirements are clearly spelled out in a *statute*, *court rule*, or *government regulation*. For example, there are laws that state, "a petition for divorce must allege the following..." If you cannot find a consumer or lawyer manual on a subject, you might be able to find a statute detailing exactly what must be done. How to use statutes is described in Chapter 3 of this book.

Advanced Research

If your legal procedure is not a simple one or if the facts of your case are unusual and do not fit the research you have done, you need to research the case law and other advanced techniques explained in Chapters 4 through 6 of this book.

LOOKING UP YOUR RIGHTS

If you are seeking to learn your legal rights in a situation or lawsuit, your research will be more detailed and you will probably need to look into *case law*.

Specialty Books

To get an overview of the subject, you should first check to see if there is a specialty book on the subject you are researching. These are described in Chapter 2.

Legal Encyclopedias

If there are no specialty books on the topic you are researching, you can start with a legal encyclopedia. Some states have their own, but other states use a national version. These are explained beginning on page 24.

Statutes and Case Law

After checking the specialty books and encyclopedias, you will have some statutes or cases that apply to your case. Next, you will need to read these to see if they are still valid or have been amended or overruled. This is explained in Chapters 3 and 4 of this book.

A QUICK NOTE ABOUT LAW BOOKS AND CITATIONS

Law books may be very different from the typical book. They are usually published with experienced legal professionals as their primary audience, and may utilize unfamiliar numbering and citation systems. In addition, judicial decisions may be published in a variety of case reporters, and both case law and statutes may be published in official or unofficial reports or codes. Although more details about these features are described in Chapters 3 and 4, for now consider the following.

You will probably see certain law books with numerals followed by "d" or "th" in their titles (e.g., N.E.2d, Ohio Jur. 3d or A.L.R.4th). These numbers typically mean one of two things—either the book replaces an older *edition*, or it is part of a *series* that reaches a certain volume number, then starts over again with volume one in a second or higher series.

Editions vs. Series

New editions generally completely replace older editions; whereas new volumes in subsequent series do not replace identically numbered volumes in prior series. For example, the book *Newberg on Class Actions 4th* replaced *Newberg on Class Actions 3rd*, while the *Northeastern Reporter (N.E.)* contains 200 volumes of early reported cases in its first series (1 N.E. through 200 N.E. covers years 1885–1936); and its second series (1 N.E.2d–) contains later reported cases (1936 on).

Citations

Although you may see citations to other types of works (e.g., multi-volume treatises and legal periodicals), typically, new researchers find citations to judicial decisions in case reporters and statutes to be the most difficult to figure out. To help you get started reading citations, here are a few examples.

- *Case Decision Citation—Pittman v. Duggan*, 84 N.E.2d 701 (Ill. App. 1949). Here, "Pittman" and "Duggan" are the party names; 84 is the volume number of the case reporter; N.E.2d is the name of the case reporter (and is the abbreviation for Northeastern Reporter, 2d series); 701 is the first page on which the *Pittman v. Duggan* decision appears in the case reporter; Ill. App. is the abbreviation for Illinois Appellate Court and specifies the specific court that issued the decision; and, 1949 is the year of the decision.

- *Statute Citation*—225 Ill. Comp. Stat. Ann. 41/1-15 (West 2004). Here, 225 refers to the chapter; Ill. Comp. Stat. Ann. is the abbreviation for the code (which is Illinois Compiled Statutes Annotated); 41/1-15 refers to the act and section number; West is the publisher; and, 2004 is the date of the code edition.

NOTE: *Proper citation rules and abbreviations can be found in a number of sources, including* ***The Bluebook, A Uniform System of Citation 18th ed., 2005*** *and* ***ALWD Citation Manual: A Professional System of Citation, 2nd ed., 2002.***

Case Reporters

Court decisions may be published in a number of different *reporters*. Reporters can contain decisions from a specific court or jurisdiction. Sometimes, court decisions may appear in multiple reporters, each printed by a separate publisher. The basic court opinion is the same in each reporter, but each publisher may add its own editorial enhancements, like summaries and headnotes.

Reporters that are published by the government (or have been designated by the government) are known as *official* reporters; all others are *unofficial* reporters. Citation rules generally indicate that you should cite to official reporters before or instead of unofficial reporters.

In the early years of this country, case reporters were often known by the names of the people who transcribed the actual case reports. These nominative reporters are usually cited with the transcriber's name included in the reporter title.

To help illustrate these points, here are some of the various reporters for decisions of the United States Supreme Court.

Years	Reporter Name	Abbreviation	Status
1790–1800	Dallas	1 U.S. (1 Dall.)	Official, Nominative
1801–1815	Cranch	5 U.S. (1 Cranch)	Official, Nominative
1816–1827	Wheaton	14 U.S. (1 Wheat.)	Official, Nominative
1828–1842	Peters	26 U.S. (1 Pet.)	Official, Nominative
1843–1860	Howard	42 U.S. (1 How.)	Official, Nominative
1861–1862	Black	66 U.S. (1 Black)	Official, Nominative
1863–1874	Wallace	68 U.S. (1 Wall.)	Official, Nominative
1875–date	U.S. Reports	U.S.	Official
1790–date	U.S. Supreme Court Reports, Lawyers' Edition	L. Ed., L. Ed.2d	Unofficial
1882–date	Supreme Court Reporter	S. Ct.	Unofficial

Statutory Code Volumes

Although you will learn more about statutes and codes in Chapter 3, a quick look at statute numbering can be helpful. Statutes published in subject arrangements (codes) are usually arranged by chapter or title, with numbers assigned to each chapter. Within each chapter there may be several (or hundreds) of individual statutes, each with identifying act or section numbers. There is a wide variety in how different state statutory codes designate their statute numbering. You should pay attention to how your particular jurisdiction's statutory code numbers its statutes. Some use "chapter," "title," or "section" designations, and may include decimal points, slashes, or dashes. The following are some examples of the various designations.

- Conn. Gen. Stat. §17b-493 (2004)
- 225 Ill. Comp. Stat. Ann. 41/1 15 (West 2004)
- Vt. Stat. Ann. Tit. 12, §2151 (2004)

You may also find when looking at statutory code volumes that a particular title, chapter, or section number is indicated as "reserved," and no statutes appear under the number. This simply means that the numbering scheme is being held to use for subsequent statutes that might be enacted in the future on a particular subject represented by the numbering.

LEGAL ENCYCLOPEDIAS

If you know very little about the topic you are researching and need a broader picture of the law, you should check a legal encyclopedia. Perhaps you are unable to develop a clear picture of your goal, or you cannot think of the words to describe your topic because you are unfamiliar with the legal terminology required. You may want to use a legal encyclopedia to assist you in beginning your research.

If you live in one of the twenty-two states with their own legal encyclopedia, you are in luck. These books summarize each area of law, and give you the statutes and important cases you need to start your research.

States with Their Own Legal Encyclopedias

California	*California Jurisprudence 3d* *Summary of California Law*
Colorado	*Colorado Law Annotated 2d*
Florida	*Florida Jurisprudence*
Georgia	*Encyclopedia of Georgia Law* *Georgia Jurisprudence*
Illinois	*Illinois Jurisprudence* *Illinois Law and Practice*
Indiana	*Indiana Law Encyclopedia*
Louisiana	*Louisiana Civil Law Treatise*

Maryland	*Maryland Law Encyclopedia*
Massachusetts	*Massachusetts Practice*
Michigan	*Michigan Law and Practice 2d*
Mississippi	*Encyclopedia of Mississippi Law* *Summary of Mississippi Law*
New Hampshire	*New Hampshire Practice*
New Jersey	*New Jersey Practice*
New York	*New York Jurisprudence 2d,* *Carmody Wait 2d*
North Carolina	*North Carolina Index 4th*
Ohio	*Ohio Jurisprudence 3d*
Pennsylvania	*Pennsylvania Law Encyclopedia*
South Carolina	*South Carolina Jurisprudence*
Tennessee	*Tennessee Jurisprudence*
Texas	*Texas Jurisprudence 3d*
Virginia	*Jurisprudence of Virginia and West Virginia*
West Virginia	*Jurisprudence of Virginia and West Virginia*

The encyclopedias geared only to a particular state, such as *Texas Jurisprudence 3d* (Tex Jur 3d), outline the law in that state. In general, use only the latest edition of state encyclopedias to avoid using materials that are obsolete.

If you do not live in one of the listed states, there are also two national legal encyclopedias—*Corpus Juris Secundum* (CJS) and *American Jurisprudence 2d* (Am Jur 2d). These explain the majority rule in the United States and, on the whole, do not take individual state peculiarities into account. There are earlier versions of both of these encyclopedias (*Corpus Juris* and *American Jurisprudence*), but it would not be worthwhile to look at them since the material is outdated.

The national encyclopedias can be good sources for beginning legal researchers because they cover very broad subject areas in some depth.

As with most encyclopedias, you can either start with the topical index (usually at the end of the set), look up your subject terms, and find the relevant volume, or go to the specific volume(s) that includes your topic and look at the table of contents under each topic entry.

Corpus Juris Secundum, *American Jurisprudence 2d*, and the state encyclopedias offer an overview of the law on a particular topic and often give references to specific court cases (this will be discussed in more detail in Chapter 4), either within the text or in footnotes. These *case citations* are frequently an excellent source of material when beginning your research.

It is important to remember, however, that encyclopedias only give the very basic, bare-bones law in a particular area. They are meant to be a starting point in legal research, not the only source of law. Legal research should never stop with a legal encyclopedia. You would miss all the fine points of the law, which are always extremely important.

Remember to write down any relevant words or phrases that you discover while reading the encyclopedia. Every new word you find could be helpful as you continue your research.

Figure 1

Waiver.

In a murder prosecution, a defendant may be deemed to have waived the defense of insanity by refusing to be examined by a psychiatrist.[69]

Codefendants.

The alleged insanity of one defendant charged with murder cannot serve to shield a codefendant from liability for the murder.[70]

b. Knowledge of Right and Wrong

Ability of the accused to distinguish right from wrong with respect to the homicide and to know the nature of the act is the most frequently applied test of sanity. One who has such ability may be responsible although he is in some other respects abnormal.

The test of mental capacity most frequently employed in determining the criminal responsibility of an accused for homicide, which is known as the *M'Naghten* rule,[71] is the capacity to distinguish right from wrong, as applied to the particular act, and to understand the nature, quality, and consequences of such act.[72]

Thus, one who at the time of the commission of a homicide, by reason of mental disease, was incapable of knowing the nature and the quality of his act, or that the act was wrong, is not criminally responsible,[73] and one who knows the nature and quality of his act and that it is wrong is criminally responsible.[74]

Where the ability to distinguish between right and wrong is the test of insanity, one who is able so to distinguish is responsible notwithstanding he has a low intelligence quotient and a mental age far below his actual age,[75] or is weak-minded or feeble-minded,[76] or is otherwise mentally abnormal or defective.[77]

c. Uncontrollable Action; Irresistible Impulse

While there is authority that to render one suffering from mental disease responsible for homicide, one must have had the ability not only to distinguish right from wrong, but also to

---

68. Ariz.—State v. Prewitt, 452 P.2d 500, 104 Ariz. 326.

69. Fla.—Christopher v. State, 416 So.2d 450.

70. Mass.—Commonwealth v. McGrath, 264 N.E.2d 667, 358 Mass. 314.

71. Fla.—Holston v. State, 208 So.2d 98.

Md.—Robinson v. State, 238 A.2d 875, 249 Md. 200, certiorari denied 89 S.Ct. 259, 393 U.S. 928, 21 L.Ed.2d 265.

Miss.—Myrick v. State, 290 So.2d 259.

72. Ariz.—State v. Steelman, 585 P.2d 1213, 120 Ariz. 301, appeal after remand 612 P.2d 475, 126 Ariz. 19, certiorari denied Steelman v. Arizona, 101 S.Ct. 287, 449 U.S. 913, 66 L.Ed.2d 141.

Cal.—People v. Perry, 234 P. 890, 195 C. 623.

Ky.—Murrell v. Commonwealth, 163 S.W.2d 1, 291 Ky. 65.

Okl.—Turner v. State, 279 P. 525, 43 Okl.Cr. 380.

Pa.—Commonwealth v. Banks, 521 A.2d 1, 513 Pa. 318, certiorari denied Banks v. Pennsylvania, 108 S.Ct. 211, 98 L.Ed.2d 162.

Tex.—Davidson v. State, 4 S.W.2d 74, 109 Tex.Cr. 251.

Wash.—State v. Carpenter, 7 P.2d 573, 166 Wash. 478.

Wis.—State v. Johnson, 290 N.W. 159, 233 Wis. 668.

73. Ala.—Manning v. State, 116 So. 360, 217 Ala. 357.

Idaho—State v. Van Vlack, 65 P.2d 736, 57 Idaho 316.

Ill.—People v. Varecha, 186 N.E. 607, 353 Ill. 52.

Iowa—State v. Maharras, 224 N.W. 537, 208 Iowa 127.

Ky.—Newsome v. Commonwealth, 154 S.W.2d 737, 287 Ky. 649.

N.J.—State v. Lynch, 32 A.2d 183.

Pa.—Commonwealth v. Santos, 119 A. 596, 275 Pa. 515.

Utah—State v. Green, 6 P.2d 177, 78 Utah 580.

Belief that marriage vow bestowed right to kill partner

Where defendant, who murdered his wife, clearly could not distinguish right and wrong with regard to his act, believing that marriage vow "till death do us part" bestowed on marital partner God-given right to kill other partner if he or she was inclined to violate marital vows, defendant was entitled to judgment of not guilty by reason of insanity, without any further hearing to determine whether he was capable of knowing or understanding nature and quality of his act.

Cal.—People v. Skinner, 217 Cal.Rptr. 685, 704 P.2d 752, 39 C.3d 765.

74. Ariz.—Foster v. State, 294 P. 268, 37 Ariz. 281.

Cal.—People v. Keaton, 296 P. 609, 211 C. 722.

N.C.—State v. Davis, 361 S.E.2d 724, 321 N.C. 52.

Or.—State v. Riley, 30 P.2d 1041, 147 Or. 89.

Pa.—Commonwealth v. Bruno, 407 A.2d 413, 268 Pa.Super. 15.

Tenn.—Davis v. State, 28 S.W.2d 993, 161 Tenn. 23.

W.Va.—State v. Evans, 117 S.E. 885, 94 W.Va. 47.

75. Cal.—People v. Perry, 234 P. 890, 195 C. 623.

Mass.—Commonwealth v. Stewart, 151 N.E. 74, 255 Mass. 9.

76. Tex.—Banks v. State, 112 S.W.2d 745, 133 Tex.Cr. 541.

77. Cal.—People v. Keaton, 296 P. 609, 211 C. 722.

Mont.—State v. Colbert, 194 P. 145, 58 Mont. 584.

Emotional instability reaction

Where defendant was accused of first-degree murder, even if his record with Marine Corps showed that he suffered from emotional instability reaction as manifested by inappropriate and sudden outbursts and acts, there was no evidence that he was laboring from defect of reason so as not to know nature and quality of his act or, if he did know, that he did not know he was doing what was wrong.

Ariz.—State v. Janovic, 417 P.2d 527, 101 Ariz. 203, certiorari denied Janovic v. Arizona, 87 S.Ct. 777, 385 U.S. 1036, 17 L.Ed.2d 683.

Grand mal seizure

Occasional grand mal seizure of defendant, with some brain atrophy that did not destroy ability to know right from wrong, did not relieve him from responsibility for murder.

Iowa—State v. Arthur, 160 N.W.2d 470.

DIGESTS

Case reporters typically contain judicial decisions published in *chronological* (by date) order, rather than by subject. To find cases on a particular subject, you can use a specific type of book called a *digest*. Case digests include small summaries of individual cases, organized under broad topics and more specific subtopics. For more on digests, see Chapter 4.

INDEXES

Actual research for both cases and statutes begins in an *index*. Indexes (or indices) in legal materials are just like any other index you may run across in nonlegal materials. They are an alphabetical listing of subject references followed by the location of that subject within the volume or volumes in which you are looking.

Look up the first word or phrase you wrote down. When you find it, make note of the location. If you cannot find the word or phrase, either go on to the next word or phrase on your list or look up a synonym of that word. Continue in this manner until you exhaust your list. Most indexes will explain at the beginning what the referenced location actually means. Consult the instructions to determine whether you are being directed to a specific topic, section, page, or volume number.

The location may not appear familiar to you. In most nonlegal materials, index locations are a page—for example, "personal injury, 10." You would go to page 10 to find information on personal injury. In many legal books, however, the location is not a page number. It may be a section number, a volume number, or even a topic (such as "Personal Injury 25"). Do not let this confuse you. Proceed to the location just as if it were a page number.

Another common mistake for first-time researchers is to find a listing in an index but not realize it is a subentry (rather than a main entry). Legal indexes are often broken down into many minor subentries. For example, under "trusts," there may be five pages of subentries. If you are looking for the entry for "trustee," be sure you have found the main listing for "trustee," not the subentry of "trustee" under "trusts" or some other entry.

CARD CATALOGS

This is one source that anyone familiar with any type of library has used before. A *card catalog* is a system in which the materials in the library are cross-referenced by author, title, and subject.

In older libraries, the catalog will be a series of index cards (hence the term *card* catalog) in index drawers. The cards for author, title, and subject will be separated. In most libraries today, however, the card catalog has been replaced by computer, but the information is generally cataloged in the same manner. (For a detailed discussion on computerized databases, see Chapter 7.)

If you know your topic, and have a list of potential words and phrases ready, you can use the subject card catalog. If you need to learn the location of a set of books, use the title catalog to obtain that location.

Be aware, however, that many law libraries do not catalog certain sets of books, such as reporters, encyclopedias, and digests, which are the books you will be using the most. If you look up certain titles, such as *Corpus Juris Secundum*, and they are not in the catalog, it will be important to ask the librarian for a map of the library with the location of these materials. You may want to ask for a tour, or perhaps the library has a *self-guided tour* you could take to familiarize yourself with the library's layout.

Practice Manuals, Specialty Books, and Law Reviews

There are many books in a law library that do not just state the law, but are designed to help you understand the law or a particular legal subject or procedure. For example, when an issue has been addressed before, legal authors will often make note of the facts and court decision in their books. Many times, these books will offer commentary that may help you plot your course with your legal problem. Other books offer sample forms that you may find helpful if you must file forms with a court. This chapter is designed to introduce you to these materials.

PRACTICE MANUALS

If your research project involves accomplishing a particular legal procedure, the best place to find out how is in a book that attorneys use to learn the procedure. These books usually contain all the forms, explanations of the procedure, and even case law. They often warn you of possible problems that can come up in the procedure.

Believe it or not, law students are not taught much about how to do specific tasks. They are taught how to think like a lawyer and to do research. It is only after law school that lawyers learn how to prepare things such as divorce petitions and copyright applications. Many books explain how these things are done.

In some states, there are *practice manuals* published by private companies. In many states, they are published by the continuing education division of the state bar association. For subjects covered by federal law, such as copyright and bankruptcy, several books (some consisting of several volumes) are available.

SPECIALTY BOOKS

Perhaps you are lucky and know exactly what area of law you need to be researching. Most law libraries can accommodate this by supplying you with a specialty book, either a *monograph* or a *treatise*. Monographs and treatises are library terms used to describe certain types of books. Other types of books that cover a single area of the law include *Restatements* and *uniform laws*.

Monographs

Monographs are books that only cover a very small portion of a subject. An example outside of the legal field would be a book discussing only the Civil War battle at Gettysburg instead of covering the entire Civil War, or a book only covering Mark Twain's *Adventures of Tom Sawyer* instead of discussing all of Mark Twain's books.

If you know the very narrow field of law you will be dealing with, you may want to consult the card catalog for a monograph.

Treatises

Treatises attempt to incorporate an entire field of law within its covers. For example, a set of books regarding the Civil War from first gunshot at Ft. Sumter to surrender at Appamattox would be a treatise, as would a book about all of Mark Twain's works.

A treatise is a very helpful tool, even if you are a novice, as long as you know with what general area of law you are dealing. If you are looking through a treatise and are having trouble locating any useful material, you may be dealing with the wrong area of law. It would be wise to begin your search in encyclopedias, cases, and statutes until you are relatively certain what area is most important to your problem. Then—and only then—should you consult a treatise.

A few well-known treatises are: *Prosser and Keeton on Torts; Calamari on Contracts; Farnsworth on Contracts; Tribe on Constitutional Law; LaFave on Criminal Law;* and, *McCormick on*

Evidence. Incidentally, you may hear someone refer to many of these well-known treatises as *hornbooks*.

Additionally, there may be many treatises devoted strictly to your particular state's laws on a specific topic. These treatises are likely to be printed by the state bar association, are usually geared toward the legal practitioner, and often include samples of forms and pleadings necessary for practice of law in that area. It would be to your advantage to look through the library's card catalog to find these books.

Restatements

Published by the *American Law Institute* (ALI), *Restatements* are sets of books on specific subject areas (i.e., torts, contracts, property, etc.) that attempt to *restate* the common law (generally case law) of the U.S. by providing rules that are accompanied by explanations and annotations (notes of cases interpreting the rules). Restatements are well-respected by courts and are often used as persuasive authority when there is no direct authority on a particular issue. Each set of Restatements has its own index.

There are Restatements on the following subjects:

- agency;
- conflict of laws;
- contracts;
- foreign relations law of the United States;
- judgments;
- law governing lawyers;
- property;
    - donative transfers;
    - landlord and tenant;
    - mortgages;

    - servitudes; and,
    - wills and other donative transfers;
- restitution;
- security;
- suretyship and guaranty;
- torts;
    - products liability;
- trusts;
    - prudent investor rule; and,
- unfair competition.

Uniform Laws

Some statutes are so important that groups may want to see similar statutes in all fifty states. To accomplish this goal, groups such as the American Law Institute and the National Conference of Commissioners on Uniform State Laws draft model (also known as uniform) legislation on various subjects (e.g., Uniform Adoption Act), and then actively promote their model in the state legislatures. The most well-known *uniform law* is the Uniform Commercial Code, which covers commercial transactions. It has been adopted by forty-nine states.

NOTE: *If a state does enact a uniform law, they will often keep much of the same statutory numbering while fitting it into the state's own numbering system. For example, Illinois enacted §2-103 of the Uniform Commercial Code as 810 ILCS 5/2 103.*

Uniform laws are published in *Uniform Laws Annotated*, a set that includes the full text of the uniform law, a list of what states have enacted all or parts of the uniform law, and notes of cases that have interpreted the law. Texts of the uniform acts and related legislation can also be found on the National Conference of Commissioners on Uniform State Laws' website, **www.nccusl.org**. A partial list of model acts and uniform laws include those listed on pages 35–38.

Model Acts

Model Class Actions Act
Model Eminent Domain Code
Model Employment Termination Act
Model Health Care Consent Act
Model Insanity Defense and Post Trial Disposition Act
Model Joint Obligations Act
Model Juvenile Court Act
Model Land Sales Practices Act
Model Metric System Procedure Act
Model Minor Student Capacity to Borrow Act
Model Penal Code
Model Periodic Payment of Judgments Act
Model Punitive Damages Act
Model Real Estate Cooperative Act
Model Real Estate Time-Share Act
Model Sentencing and Corrections Act
Model State Administrative Procedure Act
Model Statutory Construction Act
Model Surface Use and Mineral Development Accommodation Act
Model Survival and Death Act

Uniform Laws

Uniform Abortion Act
Uniform Acknowledgment Act
Uniform Act for Simplification of Fiduciary Security Transfers
Uniform Act on Intestacy, Wills and Donative Transfers
Uniform Act on Paternity
Uniform Act to Secure Attendance of Witnesses from without a State in Criminal Proceedings Uniform Adoption Act
Uniform Aircraft Financial Responsibility Act
Uniform Alcoholism and Intoxication Treatment Act
Uniform Anatomical Gift Act
Uniform Apportionment of Tort Responsibility Act
Uniform Arbitration Act
Uniform Athlete Agents Act
Uniform Audio Visual Deposition Act
Uniform Brain Death Act
Uniform Certification of Questions of Law Act
Uniform Child Custody Jurisdiction and Enforcement Act
Uniform Child Witness Testimony by Alternative Methods Act
Uniform Civil Liability for Support Act
Uniform Commercial Code
Uniform Common Interest Ownership Act
Uniform Common Trust Fund Act
Uniform Comparative Fault Act
Uniform Computer Information Transactions Act

(continued)

Uniform Condominium Act
Uniform Conflict of Laws Limitations Act
Uniform Conservation Easement Act
Uniform Construction Lien Act
Uniform Consumer Credit Code
Uniform Consumer Leases Act
Uniform Consumer Sales Practice Act
Uniform Contribution Among Tortfeasors Act
Uniform Controlled Substances Act
Uniform Correction or Clarification of Defamation Act
Uniform Crime Victims Reparations Act
Uniform Criminal Extradition Act
Uniform Criminal History Records Act
Uniform Criminal Statistics Act
Uniform Custodial Trust Act
Uniform Declaratory Judgments Act
Uniform Determination of Death Act
Uniform Disclaimer of Property Interests Act
Uniform Disposition of Community Property Rights at Death Act
Uniform Division of Income for Tax Purposes Act
Uniform Divorce Recognition Act
Uniform Dormant Mineral Interests Act
Uniform Drug Dependence Treatment and Rehabilitation Act
Uniform Durable Power of Attorney Act
Uniform Duties to Disabled Persons Act
Uniform Electronic Transactions Act
Uniform Enforcement of Foreign Judgments Act
Uniform Environmental Covenants Act
Uniform Estate Tax Apportionment Act
Uniform Exemptions Act
Uniform Extradition and Rendition Act
Uniform Facsimile Signatures of Public Officials Act
Uniform Federal Lien Registration Act
Uniform Fiduciaries Act
Uniform Foreign Money Claims Act
Uniform Foreign Money Judgments Recognition Act
Uniform Fraudulent Conveyance Act
Uniform Fraudulent Transfer Act
Uniform Gifts to Minors Act
Uniform Guardianship and Protective Proceedings Act
Uniform Health Care Decisions Act
Uniform Health Care Information Act
Uniform Information Practices Code
Uniform Interstate Arbitration of Death Taxes Act
Uniform Interstate Compromise of Death Taxes Act
Uniform Interstate Family Support Act
Uniform Land Security Interest Act
Uniform Land Transactions Act
Uniform Law on Notarial Acts
Uniform Limited Liability Company Act

Uniform Limited Partnership Act
Uniform Management of Institutional Funds Act
Uniform Management of Public Employee Retirement Systems Act
Uniform Mandatory Disposition of Detainers Act
Uniform Marital Property Act
Uniform Marketable Title Act
Uniform Marriage and Divorce Act
Uniform Mediation Act
Uniform Money Services Act
Uniform Motor Vehicle Accident Reparations Act
Uniform Multiple Person Accounts Act
Uniform Narcotic Drug Act
Uniform Nonjudicial Foreclosure Act
Uniform Nonprobate Transfers on Death Act
Uniform Parentage Act
Uniform Partnership Act
Uniform Periodic Payment of Judgments Act
Uniform Perpetuation of Testimony Act
Uniform Photographic Copies of Business and Public Records as Evidence Act
Uniform Planned Community Act
Uniform Post Conviction Procedure Act
Uniform Premarital Agreement Act
Uniform Preservation of Private Business Records Act
Uniform Pretrial Detention Act
Uniform Principal and Income Act
Uniform Probate Code
Uniform Probate of Foreign Wills Act
Uniform Prudent Investor Act
Uniform Public Assembly Act
Uniform Putative and Unknown Fathers Act
Uniform Real Property Electronic Recording Act
Uniform Reciprocal Enforcement of Support Act
Uniform Reciprocal Transfer Tax Act
Uniform Recognition of Acknowledgments Act
Uniform Residential Landlord and Tenant Act
Uniform Residential Mortgage Satisfaction Act
Uniform Rights of the Terminally Ill Act
Uniform Rules of Criminal Procedure
Uniform Rules of Evidence
Uniform Securities Act
Uniform Simplification of Fiduciary Security Transfers Act
Uniform Simplification of Land Transfers Act
Uniform Simultaneous Death Act
Uniform Single Publication Act
Uniform State Antitrust Act
Uniform Status of Children of Assisted Conception Act
Uniform Statute and Rule Construction Act
Uniform Statute of Limitations on Foreign Claims Act

(continued)

Uniform Statutory Form Power of Attorney Act
Uniform Statutory Rule Against Perpetuities
Uniform Statutory Will Act
Uniform Succession Without Administration Act
Uniform Supervision of Trustees for Charitable Purposes Act
Uniform Testamentary Additions to Trusts Act
Uniform TOD Security Registration Act
Uniform Trade Secrets Act
Uniform Transboundary Pollution Reciprocal Access Act
Uniform Transfer of Litigation Act
Uniform Transfers to Minors Act
Uniform Trustees' Powers Act
Uniform Trust Code
Uniform Trusts Act
Uniform Unclaimed Property Act
Uniform Unincorporated Nonprofit Association Act
Uniform Vendor and Purchaser Risk Act
Uniform Veterans' Guardianship Act
Uniform Victims of Crime Act
Uniform Voting by New Residents in Presidential Elections Act
Uniform Wage Withholding and Unemployment Insurance Procedure Act

LAW REVIEWS AND LEGAL PERIODICALS

While most of your research will involve only case and statute research, you will occasionally wish to get a broader view of your problem and the topic it concerns. One way to do this is to research in *law reviews* and *legal periodicals*. (See Chapter 6 on using *American Law Reports*.) If you are really lucky, there will be a recent article in a law review or in a legal periodical on the subject you are researching.

Law reviews are journals published by law schools (usually quarterly). The staff members of most law reviews are ordinarily only those law students who are in the top 10–20% of their class. These students, working under the direction of a law professor, decide which articles will be published, edit the articles as necessary, and check all quotations and citations for accuracy. There is great prestige in being a member of law review, and often those students who were on law review receive the most lucrative job offers after graduation.

These reviews print articles by law professors, attorneys, members of the judiciary, and other legal scholars on subjects of current interest.

Often, the viewpoints taken by the authors expand the boundaries of legal scholarship, frequently leading to new thinking on issues and occasionally causing change in the law itself. Law reviews may be general in nature, publishing articles on a variety of topics in each issue, or they may be dedicated to specific topics only, such as women, the environment, or estate planning.

While most law review articles are written by legal professionals, law students may be contributors to reviews as well. Articles written by students are printed after the lead articles by the scholars and are usually titled "Commentary."

NOTE: *Any article not considered a lead article will be entitled "Commentary," whether it was written by a student or a legal professional.*

Legal periodicals, on the other hand, are generally magazines and other legal-related newsletters that are not classified as law reviews. For example, the *American Bar Association* publishes a monthly magazine called the *ABA Journal.* This magazine is classified as a legal periodical. Periodicals may be published weekly, biweekly, monthly, quarterly, or annually, and are usually printed by state bar associations and other legal organizations. Frequent contributors to such periodicals include law professors, attorneys, and other legal scholars (just like law reviews), but most articles are much shorter and cover a topic of current interest to practitioners.

These articles usually discuss the routine side of law instead of the academic position. For example, an article in the state bar journal may be written about new changes to the code of criminal procedure and the practical influences those changes will have upon how lawyers will handle their clients' problems and lawsuits as a result. A law review article based on the same changes in the code of criminal procedure, on the other hand, would likely discuss the constitutional ramifications of the changes—a different point of view, but both may be useful to your research.

So, how do you find individual articles when there are literally hundreds of law reviews and legal periodicals to choose from? In many law school libraries, the law reviews and periodicals take up an entire floor. There are five methods of conducting research in law reviews and legal periodicals—two are print indexes and the other three are electronic indexes.

Index to Legal Periodicals

The *Index to Legal Periodicals* (ILP) is the oldest guide to law reviews and legal periodicals. The ILP, now published by the H.W. Wilson Co., has been printed (under different publishers) since 1886. It currently indexes approximately one thousand different reviews, magazines, journals, and other legal publications that are classified as reviews or periodicals.

The ILP is published in hardcover annually, from September to August, and is updated by a pamphlet each month except September. Each volume is separated into subject and author indexes, both of which are classified alphabetically. When searching in the subject index, which is where you would usually begin, you should start in the latest monthly update pamphlet and work your way backwards into the hardcover volumes. The names of each review or periodical are generally abbreviated. The front of each volume has a table explaining what each abbreviation represents. For example, "Marq.L.Rev." represents *Marquette Law Review*.

Current Law Index

Current Law Index (CLI) has been published since 1980, and is currently published by Gale Group, a business unit of the Thomson Corporation. Like the *Index to Legal Periodicals*, it is published annually, from January to December, and is also updated monthly. The March, June, and September issues are quarterly cumulative, and the December issue is an annual supplement. Current Law Index indexes over nine hundred law journals, legal newspapers, and specialty publications from the United States, Canada, the United Kingdom, Ireland, Australia, and New Zealand.

Necessarily, there is a great deal of overlap between CLI and ILP, but CLI does cover some reviews and periodicals that ILP does not. Current Law Index does index items a little differently than Index to Legal Periodicals, so if you look up a topic in one index and cannot find something helpful, you might consider looking it up in the other. What one index might list under "divorce," the other might list under "alimony." There is no way to tell unless you research in both indexes.

WilsonWeb

The electronic counterpart to Index to Legal Periodicals is *WilsonWeb's Index to Legal Periodicals and Books*. Available as a subscription Internet or monthly CD-ROM service, this index covers citations to both legal periodicals and books from approximately 1982. A full-text database, *Index to Legal Periodicals Full-Text*, is an enhanced subscription version of Index to Legal Periodicals and books that include the full text of articles from over two hundred periodicals from 1994 to date. A separate subscription database, *Index to Legal Periodicals Retrospective: 1918–1981*, covers citations from approximately five hundred legal periodicals.

LegalTrac

Distributed by Gale Group, a business unit of the Thomson Corporation (which also owns West Publishing), *LegalTrac* is the computer database counterpart of Current Law Index. A disadvantage of LegalTrac is that it only covers articles from 1980.

HeinOnline

A third subscription electronic source is *HeinOnline*, from William S. Hein & Co. This Internet database includes full-text articles from over seven hundred law journals and periodicals. Coverage varies by journal; however, most are available in complete runs (i.e, from Vol. 1 to at least last year's volume). For example, as of the date of this writing (2005), the *Southern Illinois University Law Journal* was available from Vol. 1 (1976) through Vol. 28 (2004). The articles are searchable by title, author, or keyword, and displayed in PDF format (so the articles appear on the screen and in print as they do in the printed volumes).

The advantage of searching electronic legal periodical indexes over the print indexes is that you do not need to go from book to book (which are published by year) looking for articles on a specific subject. You can simply type your search query in an electronic index, and it will reference all covered law reviews and legal periodicals, from the beginning year of the database coverage until the last update, in reverse chronological order (from the newest article to the oldest).

Statutes and Codes

Often, the answer to a legal question is found in a statute. Both procedural questions and questions about your rights may be answered in detail in the statutes. Once you have the statute of the subject, you can check the case law for the specifics of how the statute has been interpreted.

THE DIFFERENCE BETWEEN STATUTES AND CODES

What is the difference between a *statute* and a *code*? The terms are used interchangeably by most people. Someone will say to you, "there's a statute that prohibits that," and yet the book that contains the text of the law says "Code" on the cover. In practical terms, there really is no difference between a statute and a code. These are the laws passed by state legislatures. Some states call them statutes and other states call them codes.

There was a distinction between the two words at one time, but today (and in this book) they are generally used interchangeably. Traditionally, statutes were the laws of a state in fairly random order, and a code was simply a set of books in which the statutes were arranged according to subject. Today, even states that call their laws "statutes" group laws of the same subject together. For your purposes, the difference between a statute and a code is nothing more than semantics.

What statutes represent, however, is not just semantics. Statutes are very important to your research. If your problem is governed by a particular statute or group of statutes, you will have the legal guidelines to base all of your research. It is important, therefore, to understand how statutes come into being.

THE LEGISLATIVE PROCESS

All federal laws are enacted by *Congress*. Congress is divided into two houses—the *Senate* and the *House of Representatives*.

At the beginning of each Congressional year, a Senator or Representative may introduce a *bill*, which is a proposal for a law. Bills are numbered sequentially (1, 2, 3, etc.) and have a prefix of "S." or "H.R.," depending on whether the bill originated in the Senate (S.) or the House of Representatives (H.R.). The bill may be subject to committee hearings, lobbying efforts, and debate on the floor. If the originating house approves the bill, it is given to the other house for consideration, where it may be subject to more hearings and debate.

If the bill passes, it is sent to the *President* for signing. Once signed by the President, the bill becomes law. A bill also becomes law if the President neither signs nor vetoes the bill within ten days of receiving it. If the President vetoes a bill, it can only become law if the veto is overridden by a two-thirds majority of both the Senate and the House of Representatives. A bill that is not passed through the houses, signed, or overridden is not carried over to the next session of Congress. Someone must introduce the bill again and start the process all over.

State Law

The process of making law in each state is similar to the way laws are made in the federal government. All states have two houses in their legislatures with the exception of Nebraska, which has only one.

While the names may vary, the state houses conduct business in the same manner as the U.S. Congress.

SOURCES FOR FEDERAL STATUTES

Once a bill becomes law, it is assigned a Public Law number (e.g., P.L. 101-232) that includes the Congress number (the 101st Congress) and a chronological law number (in the example P.L. 101-232, 232 was the two hundred and thirty second bill that became law in the 101st Congress). It is then sent to the Archivist who publishes the law through the United States Government Printing Office. As each law is passed, it is printed as a *slip law*, meaning that the law is published separately and unbound. Each slip law may be just a few pages, or more likely, will be hundreds of pages long. This does not mean that the statute or statutes you need will be hundreds of pages long, however. When laws are passed, they often contain many separate statutes on the same, or similar, topics. When they are published in subject-arranged codes, they will be numbered and printed as individual statutes.

Other sources for locating new federal laws include *United States Code Congressional and Administrative News* (USCCAN), which is published by West Publishing, and *United States Code Service Advance*, published by LexisNexis (not to be confused with the advance sheets used for updating reporters discussed in Chapter 4).

Each issue of USCCAN has its own cumulative index and a *Table of Laws Enacted*. Initially, USCCAN is printed monthly in pamphlet form. It is eventually replaced at the end of the Congressional session by hardbound volumes. LexisNexis' *United States Code Service Advance* pamphlets are published monthly.

A looseleaf service that will include the text of certain laws passed during the prior week is *United States Law Weekly*. This service also prints selected cases of interest, so you may want to consider glancing at it for case research as well. (See the section on "Looseleaf Services" in Chapter 4.)

The federal government publishes *session laws*, including all the slip laws passed during a specific Congress, in an official, bound set titled "United States Statutes at Large" (also known as "Statutes at Large"). The session laws are printed chronologically, so any later amendments to the original session law will most likely appear in subsequent volumes.

The Internet offers a number of locations for accessing new (and older) federal session laws. GPO Access, a service of the U.S. Government Printing Office, offers a searchable collection of public laws from the 104th Congress (1994-1995) to the present at **www.gpoaccess.gov/plaws/index.html**. Congressional (from LexisNexis), a subscription database available at many academic and large public libraries, provides searchable, full-text access to public laws, beginning with the 100th Congress (1988).

Unless you are searching for brand-new federal laws, you will want to use the *codified versions* of the statutes. The laws of the federal government have also been *codified*, meaning classified by subject, which makes research much easier. There are three printed codified versions of the federal statutes, one published by the federal government and two by private publishers.

United States Code (U.S.C.) is the official version published by the federal government. The U.S.C. is arranged into fifty *titles*. A title is the general subject matter to which the statutes are all related.

The United States Code includes the following titles:

Title 1 General Provisions
Title 2 the Congress
Title 3 the President
Title 4 Flag and Seal, Seat of Government, and the States
Title 5 Government Organization and Employees
Title 5a Government Organization and Employees (Appendix)
Title 6 Surety Bonds [Repealed]
Title 7 Agriculture
Title 8 Aliens and Nationality
Title 9 Arbitration
Title 10 Armed Forces
Title 10a Armed Forces (Appendix)
Title 11 Bankruptcy
Title 11a Bankruptcy (Appendix)

Title 12 Banks and Banking
Title 13 Census
Title 14 Coast Guard
Title 15 Commerce and Trade
Title 16 Conservation
Title 17 Copyrights
Title 18 Crimes and Criminal Procedure
Title 18a Crimes and Criminal Procedure (Appendix)
Title 19 Customs Duties
Title 20 Education
Title 21 Food and Drugs
Title 22 Foreign Relations and Intercourse
Title 23 Highways
Title 24 Hospitals and Asylums
Title 25 Indians
Title 26 Internal Revenue Code
Title 26a Internal Revenue Code (Appendix)
Title 27 Intoxicating Liquors
Title 28 Judiciary and Judicial Procedure
Title 28a Judiciary and Judicial Procedure (Appendix)
Title 29 Labor
Title 30 Mineral Lands and Mining
Title 31 Money and Finance
Title 32 National Guard
Title 33 Navigation and Navigable Waters
Title 34 Navy [Repealed]
Title 35 Patents
Title 36 Patriotic and National Observances, Ceremonies, and Organizations
Title 37 Pay and Allowances of the Uniformed Services
Title 38 Veterans' Benefits
Title 38a Veterans' Benefits (Appendix)
Title 39 Postal Service
Title 40 Public Buildings, Property, and Works
Title 40a Public Buildings, Property, and Works (Appendix)
Title 41 Public Contracts
Title 42 the Public Health and Welfare
Title 43 Public Lands
Title 44 Public Printing and Documents
Title 45 Railroads
Title 46 Shipping
Title 46a Shipping (Appendix)
Title 47 Telegraphs, Telephones, and Radiotelegraphs
Title 48 Territories and Insular Possessions
Title 49 Transportation
Title 50 War and National Defense
Title 50a War and National Defense (Appendix)

A new edition of the U.S.C. is published every six years and updated each year with bound cumulative supplements. The U.S.C. is *unannotated*, which means it only includes the text of the statutes, and does not include editorial enhancements, such as notes of cases interpreting individual statutes.

The U.S.C. is available electronically in a number of locations. Among them are:

- GPO Access, which includes the current version of the code (2000) and the 1994 version (plus supplements), at **www.gpoaccess.gov/uscode/index.html**;
- The U.S. House of Representatives, at **http://uscode.house.gov**;
- Cornell University's Legal Information Institute, at **www.law.cornell.edu/uscode**; and,
- on **www.findlaw.com**.

The other two printed versions of codified federal laws are published by private publishers. Most lawyers and other legal professionals prefer to use these sets because they are generally more up-to-date (the government is very slow in printing the U.S.C.). Also, these unofficial sets are annotated with editorial comments and case notes, and they are better indexed.

United States Code Annotated (U.S.C.A.) is published by West Publishing Company. It is annotated and frequently makes reference to the *topic and key number system*, which is helpful when trying to find court cases pertaining to a particular statute. (See Chapter 4 for more about the topic and key number system.) There is a cumulative index at the end of the set, but each title has its own index as well.

LexisNexis publishes the *United States Code Service* (U.S.C.S.). Like U.S.C.A., U.S.C.S. is annotated and has a cumulative index at the end of the set. The U.S.C.S. can be electronically accessed at some academic libraries and larger public libraries via *Congressional* (from LexisNexis), a subscription database.

Both U.S.C.A. and U.S.C.S. are updated by monthly pamphlets, annual *pocket parts*, (in the back of each volume), and total replacement of outdated volumes when necessary.

SOURCES FOR STATE STATUTES

There is little uniformity between the statutes of the various states. Most states publish slip laws, but a few do not, and the indexing is inconsistent.

There is one feature that is typical for all states, however, and that is the *session law*. All states publish session laws at the end of each legislative session. Session laws are printed chronologically, usually in pamphlet form. These pamphlets may be the only avenue to find new state laws before they are formally printed in hardbound sets of statutes or codes. Indexes are usually found at the end of each pamphlet and only cover the materials in that pamphlet, although some states will publish a cumulative index as well. They may also include a table by statute number that tells you if that particular statute has been changed and which session law contains those changes.

All states have statutes or codes. However, there is little uniformity between the states as to how they are set out or indexed. Research in one state will not necessarily correspond to research in another state.

Some states have unannotated official statutes, but a few annotate their own. Most states rely entirely on private publishers to print their statutes and codes. Unlike the reporter system, however, most states sanction these volumes as proper authority for state law when there is not an official set. All states have an annotated set of statutes, which are published by private companies.

Use your library's online (or card) catalog to find the annotated codes for your state. Most states have just one, but a few have two or more versions (from different publishers). For example, Illinois offers *West's Smith-Hurd Illinois Compiled Statutes Annotated* and *Illinois Compiled Statutes Annotated* (LexisNexis).

Individual state statutes and session laws can generally be quickly found on the Internet, using one of the following websites:

- *The National Conference of State Legislatures*—**www.ncsl.org/public/leglinks.cfm** (includes state legislature Internet links to statutes);

- *The Law Library of Congress U.S. States and Territories*—**www.loc.gov/law/guide/usstates.html** (includes legislative links for each individual state);

- Full-Text State Statutes and Legislation on the Internet—**www.prairienet.org/~scruffy/f.htm**;

- State and Local Government on the Net, State Legislatures—**www.statelocalgov.net/50states-legislature.cfm**; and,

- *State Capital* (LexisNexis), a subscription database that can be accessed at some academic libraries and larger public libraries, offers keyword searchable state statutes.

HOW TO FIND A STATUTE

There are several ways to find a particular statute. Most Internet sites that offer statutes have some mechanism for subject or keyword searching. Consult the *Help* or *Frequently Asked Questions* (FAQ) section of the site for more information on how to search. In addition, many sites allow you to view the table of contents for the entire statutory code, and then choose a specific section or subsection. Two other methods of finding statutes are using an index and the popular name table.

Indexes

Statutes may be found directly through an index. Statutes and codes for each state have at least one index volume. Following the guidelines in Chapter 1, you should start your research by thinking of all possible words and phrases pertaining to your problem. For example, if you are looking for laws concerning alimony, you should think of—in addition to the word "alimony"—the words "support" and "divorce." Use these words to begin your search of the index. (see Figure 2, page 52.) Notice that the index does not lead you to a page number, but to a statute number.

You may find it tempting to go directly to a code if you think you know which title or chapter applies to your problem. In fact, it will probably be in your best interest to look through the general or cumulative index first, if for no other reason than to confirm your suspicions. Sometimes you will find that the code you thought was the right one turns out not to be. An important rule of legal research is to avoid wasting time and effort. Spend the extra few minutes looking through the index. Those minutes may save you hours in the long run.

There is no comprehensive way to look up statutes in multiple jurisdictions. (However, some treatises or even self-help law books may have summaries of the law in various states.) If you must find out details of the law in more than one state, you will have to search each state individually. Additionally, since not all state statutes and codes are published by West Publishing, there is not the degree of uniformity that there is when researching case law. There is no guarantee that what you found in the Michigan index under "Divorce" will be under "Divorce" in the New Hampshire index.

Popular Name Tables

Sometimes a statute will be commonly known by a name, such as *COBRA* (*Consolidated Omnibus Budget Reconciliation Act*) or *The Lemon Law*. You may find these through a popular name table that is often appended as a separate volume of the statute books themselves (or appears in the last volume of the statute index). *Shepard's Citations* (discussed in Chapter 5) also has volumes devoted to popular names, titled *Shepard's Acts and Cases by Popular Names*. In this set, if the name of the law is used by more than one jurisdiction, it is listed first by the federal law and then by state law. (see Figure 3, page 53.)

Figure 2

MARRIAGE

130

Figure 3

FEDERAL AND STATE ACTS CITED BY POPULAR NAME — Una

U

U C D Act (Disability)
Cal. Unemployment Insurance Code § 2601 et seq.

U-Drive-It Act
N.J. Stat. Ann., 45:21-1 et seq.

UCC Fee and Corporation Bureau Law
Pa. Cons. Stat., Title 15, § 151 et seq.

Uintah and Ouray Reservation Termination Act of 1954
Aug. 27, 1954, Ch. 1009, 68 Stat. 868, 25 U.S. Code §§ 677 to 677aa
Aug. 2, 1956, Ch. 880, 70 Stat. 936, 25 U.S. Code §§ 677d, 677g, 677p
Sept. 25, 1962, P.L. 87-698, 76 Stat. 597, 25 U.S. Code § 677i

Ulster County Resource Recovery Agency Act
N.Y. Public Authorities Law (Consol. Laws Ch. 43A) § 2050a et seq.

Ulster Site Development Law
N.Y. Local Laws 1971, Town of Ulster, p. 3552

Ultimate Street Improvements Act
N.C. Private Laws 1927, Ch. 156

Umatilla Basin Project Act
Oct. 28, 1988, P.L. 100-557, 102 Stat. 2791

Umatilla Herd Law
Ore. Code 1930, §§ 20-2077 to 20-2084

Umstead Act (Government Sale of Merchandise)
N.C. Gen. Stat. 1943, § 66-58

UMTA
See Urban Mass Transportation Act of 1964

Unattended Motor Vehicle Act
S.C. Code Ann. 1976, § 56-5-2570

Unauthorized Attorney Compensation Act
Tex. Government Code, § 84.001 et seq.

Unauthorized Companies Act
Pa. Purdon's Stat., Title 72, §§ 2265, 2266

Unauthorized Compensation Law (Attorney)
Tex. Government Code, § 84.001 et seq.

Unauthorized Domestic Insurers Act
N.C. Gen. Stat. 1943, § 58-14-1 et seq.

Unauthorized Harvesting of Timber Act
Tex. Natural Resources Code, § 151.101 et seq.

Unauthorized Insurance Process Law
Fla. Stat. Ann., 626.904 et seq.

Unauthorized Insurance Regulation Act
Colo. Rev. Stat., 10-3-901 et seq.

Unauthorized Insurers Act
See Uniform Unauthorized Insurers Act
Conn. Gen. Stat. 1983, § 38-263 et seq.
Ind. Code 1982, 37-4-4-1 et seq.
Neb. Rev. Stat. 1943, 44-2001 to 44-2008
N.M. Stat. Ann., 59A-15-21 et seq.
W. Va. Code 1966, § 33-3-18 et seq.

Unauthorized Insurers False Advertising Process Act
Cal. Insurance Code § 1620.1 et seq.
Ida. Code 1947, 41-1235 et seq.
Ill. Rev. Stat. 1991, Ch. 73, § 735.1
Ind. Code Ann., 27-4-6-1 et seq.
Kan. Stat. Ann., 40-2415 et seq.
La. Rev. Stat. Ann., 22:1231 et seq.
Md. Ann. Code 1957, Art. 48A, § 235 et seq.
Md. Ann. Code 1974, Art. IN, § 27-701 et seq.
Me. Rev. Stat. Ann. 1964, Title 24-A, § 2102, 2109 et seq.
Minn. Stat. Ann., 72A.33 et seq.
N.C. Gen. Stat. 1943, § 58-29-1 et seq.
N.D. Cent. Code, 26-09.1-01 et seq.
Neb. Rev. Stat. 1943, 44-1801 et seq.
Nev. Rev. Stat. 1979 Reprint, 685B.090 et seq.

Continued

ANNOTATIONS

As mentioned, both the U.S.C.A. and U.S.C.S. are annotated, as are all state statutes published by private companies. *Annotations* are abstracts, or summaries, about cases construing a particular point of law. These cases interpret the statute you are researching.

You will find the abstract or abstracts directly after the text of the statute. On occasion, there may be enough abstracts concerning a particular statute to take up ten, twenty, maybe even one hundred pages. Do you read all the pages? Not necessarily. Usually, there is a small table of contents for the abstracts. (In West publications they are called *Notes of Decisions*.) The tables of contents will refer you to a number, and that number will refer to the place where the annotations for that very specific point begin. (see Figure 4, p.56.)

Once you look through the annotations pertaining to your statute, you can begin your case research (if you have not already). If you have already done some research in the digests, the annotations in the code or statutes may lead you to cases you had not discovered before.

Even if you think you have enough cases to work with, look through the annotations anyway. You may find a case that construes the statute you are using exactly. That would open up your research again, but you should not consider that a failure. Often, good legal research requires backtracking over what appears to be the same steps. Anytime you find something else that is helpful, you are ahead of the game.

ADMINISTRATIVE LAW

In addition to finding statutes, you may need to research administrative regulations and agency decisions. The following sections describe both types of legal authority and provide sources for locating them.

Regulations

Regulations are rules that are *promulgated*, or declared, by a state or federal agency. All regulations, whether state or federal, are promulgated in essentially the same manner. (The method is described in the section on federal regulations on page 57.)

Federal Register

There are many federal agencies. Some you have probably heard of include the Internal Revenue Service (IRS), the Federal Aviation

Administration (FAA), and the Federal Communications Commission (FCC). These agencies, as well as all of the others, have many rules and regulations that they use to regulate any business or organization that comes under their jurisdiction. For example, just think about all of those tax rules that you deal with each year when tax season arrives. The IRS gets the authority to promulgate these rules from Congress (although technically, all agencies fall under the Executive Branch of government, namely the President).

When Congress passes a law, it includes a short statement that says something to the effect that it authorizes "any and all other rules and regulations as may be required." This very vague and general turn of words allows the agency involved to write any rule or regulation it deems necessary to enforce the law that Congress passed. There are only two ways a regulation may be stopped. One is if Congress removes the power from the agency; for example, if the Internal Revenue Service requires that all taxpayers must file a quarterly return and Congress passes a law stating that no taxpayer must file a quarterly return, the regulation is no longer to be enforceable. The other is if a court determines that the rule is unfair or unconstitutional, and commands the agency to *cease and desist* trying to enforce it.

When a regulation is first promulgated by a federal agency, it is published in the *Federal Register*. (see Figure 5 on page 60.) The *Federal Register* is published in softcover form daily, excluding Saturdays, Sundays, and federal holidays. Pages are numbered sequentially throughout the year. Each issue in a year is considered part of one volume; for example, all issues for 2005 are part of Volume 70.

How do you find new regulations in any given year when there are approximately three hundred issues, comprising of more than fifty thousand pages, per year? Each issue contains a table of contents and an index, but that would still be an unmanageable way to do research. (see Figure 6, p.61.) There are two aids to help you in this process, however. One is called the *List of CFR Sections Affected* (L.S.A.), which is discussed on page 57. The other is the *CFR Parts Affected*. This is published in each issue of the *Federal Register*. You should check the last issue for each month following the last LSA update. For example, if the last L.S.A. is June and it is now September, you need to look in the last *Federal Register* issue for July, August, and the last *Federal Register* for September that is on the library shelf.

Figure 4

8. Evidence

Evidence supported trial court's equitable distribution of marital assets giving 50% of husband's military pension to former wife and awarding permanent periodic alimony. Brooks v. Brooks, App. 2 Dist., 602 So.2d 630 (1992).

It is responsibility of counsel to present trial court with sufficient, detailed evidence concerning retirement plans so that it can accomplish equitable distribution; trial court cannot meet its burden if parties fail to provide such information as is required to support distinction between marital and nonmarital assets and to determine proper valuations. Glover v. Glover, App. 1 Dist., 601 So.2d 231 (1992), opinion clarified.

9. Remand

Final judgment of dissolution had to be remanded for consideration of wife's pension on equitable distribution scheme for marital assets. Eady v. Eady, App. 1 Dist., 624 So.2d 360 (1993).

61.08. Alimony

(1) In a proceeding for dissolution of marriage, the court may grant alimony to either party, which alimony may be rehabilitative or permanent in nature. In any award of alimony, the court may order periodic payments or payments in lump sum or both. The court may consider the adultery of either spouse and the circumstances thereof in determining the amount of alimony, if any, to be awarded. In all dissolution actions, the court shall include findings of fact relative to the factors enumerated in subsection (2) supporting an award or denial of alimony.

(2) In determining a proper award of alimony or maintenance, the court shall consider all relevant economic factors, including but not limited to:

(a) The standard of living established during the marriage.

(b) The duration of the marriage.

(c) The age and the physical and emotional condition of each party.

(d) The financial resources of each party, the nonmarital and the marital assets and liabilities distributed to each.

(e) When applicable, the time necessary for either party to acquire sufficient education or training to enable such party to find appropriate employment.

(f) The contribution of each party to the marriage, including, but not limited to, services rendered in homemaking, child care, education, and career building of the other party.

(g) All sources of income available to either party.

The court may consider any other factor necessary to do equity and justice between the parties.

(3) To the extent necessary to protect an award of alimony, the court may order any party who is ordered to pay alimony to purchase or maintain a life insurance policy or a bond, or to otherwise secure such alimony award with any other assets which may be suitable for that purpose.

(4)(a) With respect to any order requiring the payment of alimony entered on or after January 1, 1985, unless the provisions of paragraph (c) or paragraph (d) apply, the court shall direct in the order that the payments of alimony be made through the appropriate depository as provided in s. 61.181.

(b) With respect to any order requiring the payment of alimony entered before January 1, 1985, upon the subsequent appearance, on or after that date,

The *Federal Register* may also be accessed electronically through GPO Access at **www.gpoaccess.gov/fr/index.html**, and includes volumes 59 (1994) to the present volume. A comprehensive collection of the *Federal Register* (volumes 1–65, 1936–2000) can be found on *HeinOnline*, a subscription electronic source from William S. Hein & Co., which is available at many academic law libraries.

Code of Federal Regulations

The *Code of Federal Regulations* (C.F.R.) is the codified set of all regulations. It consists of softbound pamphlets covering fifty titles. (see Figure 7 on page 62.) These titles are substantially the same as those in the *United States Code*. They are updated quarterly by title. Titles 1–16 are updated January 1st of each year, titles 17–27 by April 1st, titles 28–41 by July 1st, and titles 42–50 by October 1st. A typical citation to the C.F.R. contains the title number, part and section number, and year. For example, 21 C.F.R.130.11 (2005) refers to title 21 (Food and Drugs), 130 is the part number, and .11 is the section number (which refers to label designations of ingredients for standardized foods).

The Code of Federal Regulations has multiple methods of aiding you in researching agency regulations. There is an index at the end of each title, as well as a cumulative index volume at the end of the set. This separate index, titled "CFR Index and Finding Aids," includes a helpful table, called the "Parallel Table of Authorities and Rules," that cross-references enabling statute citations with corresponding regulations. (see Figure 8 on page 63.) In addition, there is the *List of CFR Sections Affected* (L.S.A.). This is printed monthly and lists all new regulations promulgated since the last C.F.R. The L.S.A. will note the volume and page in the Federal Register of each C.F.R. section changed. (see Figures 9 and 10 on pages 64–65.)

The Code of Federal Regulations may also be accessed electronically through GPO Access at **www.gpoaccess.gov/cfr/index.html**, and includes volumes for 1996 through 2005. Alternatively, you can also access the current version of C.F.R. through Cornell University's Legal Information Institute at **cfr.law.cornell.edu/cfr**.

Agency Decisions

Many administrative agencies are also responsible for issuing decisions that interpret its own rules and regulations, or determine a specific party's eligibility for, or proper usage of, an agency program or service. Examples include the Internal Revenue Service (IRS) deciding to allow a taxpayer a proposed exemption, the National Labor Relations Board (NLRB) interpreting its rules on union picketing, or the Social Security Administration (SSA) upholding the denial of a claim for payment. Although agency decisions are more like case law (see Chapter 4), than statutes, they are discussed in this section because of their direct connection to administrative regulations. You may need to research administrative agency decisions to see how an agency construes its regulations or to see if an agency is properly following the authority it was given by Congress.

Publication and indexing of federal agency decisions vary widely. Some agencies (e.g., the Federal Trade Commission and the Department of the Interior) have been publishing printed decisions for decades (and many academic law libraries collect them). Others may not be as widely available, and thus, may be harder to find. Check your library's online catalog to see what federal administrative agency decisions they own.

Many federal agencies now make their administrative decisions available on their agency websites. Also, LSU Libraries offer a searchable Federal Agencies Directory at **www.lib.lsu.edu/gov/fedgov.html**, and the University of Virginia Library offers an extensive listing of federal administrative decisions on the Internet at **www.lib.virginia.edu/govdocs/fed_decisions_agency.html**.

State Sources

There is no uniformity to the publication and researching of state regulations and agency decisions. Some states have complete administrative codes and registers, others may only offer registers or expect individual agencies to publish their own regulations. The publications may be in looseleaf, pamphlet, or bound volume formats, or may only be available on the Internet. Updating may be weekly, monthly, quarterly, or even annually, and indexing may be spotty.

This is most definitely an area where you should consult a reference librarian if you need to research state administrative law. It should be noted that many law libraries may only carry the regulations (and possibly agency decisions) for the state in which they are located.

More and more states are making their regulations available on the Internet. There are several websites that provide links to all fifty states' legal authority, including any administrative rules and regulations. To determine whether your states' regulations are online, consult one of the following.

- Cornell University's Legal Information Institute's *Law by Source-State* Web page (listing by Jurisdiction)—**www.law.cornell.edu/states/listing.html**.

- The Law Library of Congress' *U.S. States and Territories* Web page—**www.loc.gov/law/guide/usstates.html**, which provides individual links to each state, further subdivided by subject (look under "Executive" for administrative regulations).

- *FindLaw* offers links to state regulations through its general page on U.S. States, Cases, Codes, Statutes, and Regulations—**www.findlaw.com/casecode**.

- *State Capital* (LexisNexis), a subscription database that can be accessed at some academic libraries and larger public libraries, offers keyword searchable state administrative codes and registers.

State Agency Decisions. Publication of state agency decisions vary widely by state. Check your library's online catalog to determine whether published decisions for the agency you are interested in are available; otherwise, call the agency. Once you locate published decisions for the agency, check for possible subject or keyword indexing. Many state agencies are now placing their administrative decisions on their agency website, so it might be a good idea to look there first. There is a listing of state and local agencies and offices by topic available *FirstGov.gov*, at **www.firstgov.gov/Agencies/State_and_Territories/.shtml**. Keep in mind, however, that most agency decisions on the Web will only cover at most the last five to ten years, as agencies typically do not have the resources to scan older decisions and make them available electronically. However, some academic law schools have taken on the task of making state agency decisions publicly available via the Internet. Rutgers University, Camden, offers New Jersey administrative law decisions from 1997 to date at **www.lawlibrary.rutgers.edu/oal/search.html**.

Figure 5

41822 Federal Register / Vol. 70, No. 138 / Wednesday, July 20, 2005 / Rules and Regulations

DEPARTMENT OF AGRICULTURE

Federal Crop Insurance Corporation

7 CFR Part 400

RIN 0563–AB95

General Administrative Regulations, Subpart V—Submission of Policies, Provisions of Policies, Rates of Premium, and Premium Reduction Plans

AGENCY: Federal Crop Insurance Corporation, USDA.

ACTION: Interim rule.

SUMMARY: The Federal Crop Insurance Corporation (FCIC) amends the General Administrative Regulations to include provisions regarding the requests by approved insurance providers to implement the premium reduction plan authorized under section 508(e)(3) of the Federal Crop Insurance Act (Act) and the approval of the amount of a premium discount to be provided to farmers under the premium reduction plan.

DATES: Effective June 30, 2005.

FOR FURTHER INFORMATION CONTACT: For further information, contact Lee Ziegler, Economist, Reinsurance Services Division, Risk Management Agency, United States Department of Agriculture, 1400 Independence Avenue, Room 6739–S, Washington, DC 20250; telephone number (202) 720–0191, e-mail address: *lee.ziegler@rma.usda.gov.*

SUPPLEMENTARY INFORMATION:

Executive Order 12866

This rule has been determined to be not significant for the purposes of Executive Order 12866.

Paperwork Reduction Act of 1995

In accordance with the Paperwork Reduction Act of 1995 (44 U.S.C. Chapter 35), RMA's request for emergency approval on a new information collection, Premium Reduction Plan, was approved under OMB control number 0563–0079.

Government Paperwork Elimination Act (GPEA) Compliance

In its efforts to comply with GPEA, FCIC requires all approved insurance providers delivering the crop insurance program to make all insurance documents available electronically and to permit producers to transact business electronically. Further, to the maximum extent practicable, FCIC transacts its business with approved insurance providers electronically.

Unfunded Mandates Reform Act of 1995

Title II of the Unfunded Mandates Reform Act of 1995 (UMRA) establishes requirements for Federal agencies to assess the effects of their regulatory actions on State, local, and tribal governments and the private sector. This rule contains no Federal mandates (under the regulatory provisions of title II of the UMRA) for State, local, and tribal governments or the private sector. Therefore, this rule is not subject to the requirements of sections 202 and 205 of UMRA.

Executive Order 13132

It has been determined under section 1(a) of Executive Order 13132, Federalism, that this rule does not have sufficient implications to warrant consultation with the states. The provisions contained in this rule will not have a substantial direct effect on states, on the relationship between the national government and the states, or on the distribution of power and responsibilities among the various levels of government.

Regulatory Flexibility Act

FCIC certifies that this regulation will not have a significant economic impact on a substantial number of small entities. This action does not increase the burden on any entity because it merely clarifies the process to submit premium reduction plans to the FCIC Board of Directors for approval. The current requirements of the Standard Reinsurance Agreement (SRA) and procedures for premium reduction plans approved by the Board contain provisions to ensure that small entities have access to policies and plans of insurance, including premium reduction plans. The requirement to apply for a premium reduction plan is the same for small entities as it is for large entities. A Regulatory Flexibility Analysis has not been prepared since this regulation does not have an impact on small entities, and, therefore, this regulation is exempt from the provisions of the Regulatory Flexibility Act (5 U.S.C. 605).

Federal Assistance Program

This program is listed in the Catalog of Federal Domestic Assistance under No. 10.450.

Executive Order 12372

This program is not subject to the provisions of Executive Order 12372, which require intergovernmental consultation with State and local officials. See the Notice related to 7 CFR part 3015, subpart V, published at 48 FR 29115, June 24, 1983.

Executive Order 12988

This rule has been reviewed in accordance with Executive Order 12988 on civil justice reform. The provisions of this rule will not have a retroactive effect. The provisions of this rule will preempt State and local laws to the extent such State and local laws are inconsistent herewith, unless otherwise specified in the rule. The appeals procedures at 7 CFR 400.169 and 7 CFR part 24 must be exhausted before any action against FCIC for judicial review may be brought.

Environmental Evaluation

This action is not expected to have a significant economic impact on the quality of the human environment, health, and safety. Therefore, neither an Environmental Assessment nor an Environmental Impact Statement is needed.

Background

On February 24, 2005, FCIC published a notice of proposed rulemaking in the **Federal Register** at 70 FR 9001–9013 to revise 7 CFR part 400, subpart V, Submission of Policies, Provisions of Policies, Rates of Premium, and Premium Reduction Plans. Following publication of the proposed rule, the public was afforded 60 days to submit written comments and opinions. Approximately 1,900 comments were received from approved insurance providers, farmers, agents and other interested parties.

After consideration of all the comments and the concerns expressed, FCIC realizes it needs to proceed cautiously to ensure the continued access of farmers to crop insurance and stability of the delivery system for the federal crop insurance program. Not publishing a rule is not an option because section 508(e)(3) of the Act states that FCIC shall consider all applications of the approved insurance providers to participate in the premium reduction plan. To allow such application without ensuring that premium reduction plans are fair and equitable and do not endanger the delivery system would jeopardize the program far more than implementing a rule intended to protect these principles.

However, to allow itself the maximum flexibility in quickly making changes to the rule, should they become necessary, FCIC has elected to publish this rule as an interim rule. All the comments provided in response to the proposed rule were considered when developing

Figure 6

Centers

Medicare and medicaid:
Outpatient drugs and biologicals under part B; competitive acquisition, 39022

PROPOSED RULES

Medicaid:
Hospice care; participation conditions, 30840
Hospital participation conditions; standards for certification, 15266
Organ procurement organizations; coverage requirements, 6086
Medicare:
Conditions for coverage for end-stage renal disease facilities, 6184
Electronic Prescription Drug Program; voluntary Medicare prescription drug benefit, 6256
Home health prospective payment system; 2006 CY rates update, 40788
Hospice care; participation conditions, 30840
Hospice wage index (2006 FY), 22394
Hospital inpatient prospective payment systems and 2006 FY rates, 23306
Hospital outpatient prospective payment system and 2006 FY rates, 42674
Hospital participation conditions; standards for certification, 15266
Inpatient rehabilitation facility prospective payment system (2006 FY); update, 30188
Long-term care hospitals; prospective payment system; annual payment rate updates and policy changes, 5724
Medicare Integrity Program; fiscal intermediary and carrier functions, and conflict of interest requirements, 35204
Organ procurement organizations; coverage requirement, 6086, 15265
Organ transplant centers; hospital participation conditions; approval requirements, 6140, 15264
Outpatient drugs and biologicals; competitive acquisition under Part B, 10746
Skilled nursing facilities; prospective payment system and consolidated billing; update, 29070

NOTICES

Agency information collection activities; proposals, submissions, and approvals, 91, 1446, 3530, 3531, 4127, 4128, 5686, 7276, 7277, 8375, 8376, 9335, 10644, 12220, 12221, 13507, 17093, 17094, 20123, 20916, 21198, 21199, 22315, 22317, 24048, 25578, 29313, 29314, 30730, 32630, 32631, 35253, 35254, 35255, 35256, 36612, 36613, 39513, 41034, 42324, 42325, 42326, 43885
Clinical Laboratory Improvements Amendments programs:
Laboratories, licensed; exemptions—
Washington, 22317
National accreditation organizations; approval—
American Society for Hitocompatibility and Immunogenetics, 15327
Committees; establishment, renewal, termination, etc.:
Ambulatory Payment Classification Groups Advisory Panel, 9336, 18028
Medicaid Commission, 29765
Medicare Coverage Advisory Committee, 42327
Medicare Education Advisory Panel, 4129, 20916, 42328
Grants and cooperative agreements; availability, etc.:
Medicaid—
All-inclusive elderly care program; private, for-profit demonstration project; withdrawal cancellation, 9337
Medicare—
All-inclusive elderly care program; private, for-profit demonstration project; withdrawal cancellation, 9337
Medical Adult Day-Care Services Demonstration Program, 36613
Rural Hospice Demonstration, 17697
State Children's Health Insurance Program (2006 FY), 36615
State Children's Health Insurance Program; unexpended (2002 FY) allotments redistribution, 3036
Health Insurance Portability and Accountability Act; non-compliance complaints; filing and review procedures, 15329
Medicaid:
National accreditation organizations; approval—
American Osteopathic Association, 15333
American Society for Hitocompatibility and Immunogenetics, 15327
Community Health Accreditation Program, 15335
Joint Commission on Accreditation of Healthcare Organizations, 15331
Program issuances and coverage decisions; quarterly listing, 9338, 36620
Medicare:
Ambulatory surgical centers; new technology intraocular lenses; payment review, 30731
Clinical diagnostic laboratory services; negotiated national coverage determinations; code list maintenance procedures, 9355
Durable medical equipment regional service areas; geographical boundaries changes, 9358
Inpatient rehabilitation facility classification criteria, 36640
In-State quality improvement organization contracts; statements of interest solicitation from various States, 6012
Medicare Prescription Drug, Improvement, and Modernization Act of 2003, implementation—
Chiropractic services; coverage demonstration, 4130
Oxygen and oxygen equipment; 2005 monthly payments amounts, 6013
National accreditation organizations; approval—
American Osteopathic Association, 15333
American Society for Hitocompatibility and Immunogenetics, 15327
Community Health Accreditation Program, 15335
Joint Commission on Accreditation of Healthcare Organizations, 15331
New technology intraocular lenses furnished by ambulatory surgical centers; payment amount adjustments; disapproval, 15337
Part D reinsurance payment demonstration, 9360
Program issuances and coverage decisions; quarterly listing, 9338, 36620
Supplemental insurance regulation; National Association of Insurance Commissioners model standards, 15393
Meetings:
Emergency Medical Treatment and Labor Act Technical Advisory Group, 12691, 28541
Medicaid Commission, 40039
Medicare—
Ambulatory Payment Classification Groups Advisory Panel, 39514, 40709
Clinical laboratory tests; Physicians' Current Procedural Terminology codes, 30734
Demonstration of Bundled Case-Mix Adjusted Payment System for End-Stage Renal Disease Services Advisory Board, 4132, 15343, 19090, 22320, 36642
Healthcare Common Procedure Coding System; coding and payment determinations, 15340
Medicare Coverage Advisory Committee, 4133, 15341, 42329
Medicare Education Advisory Panel, 9362, 10645, 30733
Practicing Physicians Advisory Council, 6014, 22321, 42330
Organization, functions, and authority delegations:
External Affairs Office et al., 30735
Succession order, 42331
Privacy Act:
Computer matching programs, 42558
System of records, 2637
Systems of records, 38944, 41035
Reports and guidance documents; availability, etc.:
Medicare program; evaluation criteria and standards for quality improvement program contracts, 42331
Applications, hearings, determinations, etc.:
Indiana Medicaid State plan amendment; disapproval reconsideration, 1719

Central Intelligence Agency

NOTICES

Privacy Act:
Systems of records, 29832, 42418
Reports and guidance documents; availability, etc.:
Fleet alternative fuel use and vehicle acquisition report (2004 and 2005 FY), 40688

Central Security Service/National Security Agency

See National Security Agency/Central Security Service

Chemical Safety and Hazard Investigation Board

NOTICES

Meetings; Sunshine Act, 4090, 7924, 9611, 23980

Children and Families Administration

See Refugee Resettlement Office

PROPOSED RULES

Foster care (Title IV-E) eligibility and administrative cost provisions, 4803

NOTICES

Agency information collection activities; proposals, submissions, and approvals, 1896, 1897, 2410, 2411, 2641, 3532, 3533, 3710, 3933, 5451, 7507, 7745, 7746, 8093, 9081, 10646, 11986, 12491, 13508, 13510, 14696, 14697, 15862, 19762, 20374, 20375, 20376, 20377, 20917, 20918, 21203, 22662, 28542, 29314, 29315, 29316, 29317, 29318, 29767, 32782, 32783, 34130, 34774, 35257, 36642, 36941, 37411, 37412, 37413, 40370, 40371, 40709, 41039, 41040, 42562, 43435, 43436, 43886
Grant and cooperative agreement awards:
A+ for Abstinence, et al., 36399
Bilateral Safety Corridor Coalition of San Diego, CA, et al., 29527

8 **FEDERAL REGISTER INDEX, January--July 2005**

Figure 7

(d) *Certification.* All batches of FD&C Yellow No. 6 shall be certified in accordance with regulations in part 80 of this chapter.

[51 FR 41782, Nov. 19, 1986, as amended at 52 FR 21508, June 8, 1987; 53 FR 49138, Dec. 6, 1988]

§ 74.1707 D&C Yellow No. 7.

(a) *Identity.* (1) The color additive D&C Yellow No. 7 is principally fluorescein.

(2) Color additive mixtures for use in externally applied drugs made with D&C Yellow No. 7 may contain only those diluents that are suitable and that are listed in part 73 of this chapter for use in color additive mixtures for coloring externally applied drugs.

(b) *Specifications.* D&C Yellow No. 7 shall conform to the following specifications and shall be free from impurities other than those named to the extent that such impurities may be avoided by good manufacturing practice:

Sum of water and chlorides and sulfates (calculated as sodium salts), not more than 6 percent.
Matter insoluble in alkaline water, not more than 0.5 percent.
Resorcinol, not more than 0.5 percent.
Phthalic acid, not more than 0.5 percent.
2-2,4-(Dihydroxybenzoyl) benzoic acid, not more than 0.5 percent.
Lead (as Pb), not more than 20 parts per million.
Arsenic (as As), not more than 3 parts per million.
Mercury (as Hg), not more than 1 part per million.
Total color, not less than 94 percent.

(c) *Uses and restrictions.* D&C Yellow No. 7 may be safely used in externally applied drugs in amounts consistent with good manufacturing practice.

(d) *Labeling.* The label of the color additive and any mixtures prepared therefrom intended solely or in part for coloring purposes shall conform to the requirements of § 70.25 of this chapter.

(e) *Certification.* All batches of D&C Yellow No. 7 shall be certified in accordance with regulations in part 80 of this chapter.

§ 74.1707a Ext. D&C Yellow No. 7.

(a) *Identity.* (1) The color additive Ext. D&C Yellow No. 7 is principally the disodium salt of 8-hydroxy-5,7-dinitro-2-naphthalenesulfonic acid.

(2) Color additive mixtures for drug use made with Ext. D&C Yellow No. 7 may contain only those diluents that are suitable and that are listed in part 73 of this chapter as safe for use in color additive mixtures for coloring externally applied drugs.

(b) *Specifications.* Ext. D&C Yellow No. 7 shall conform to the following specifications and shall be free from impurities, other than those named, to the extent that such other impurities may be avoided by good manufacturing practice:

Sum of volatile matter (at 135 °C) and chlorides and sulfates (calculated as sodium salts), not more than 15 percent.
Water-insoluble matter, not more than 0.2 percent.
1-Naphthol, not more than 0.2 percent.
2,4-Dinitro-1-naphthol, not more than 0.03 percent.
Lead (as Pb), not more than 20 parts per million.
Arsenic (as As), not more than 3 parts per million.
Mercury (as Hg), not more than 1 part per million.
Total color, not less than 85 percent.

(c) *Uses and restrictions.* Ext. D&C Yellow No. 7 may be safely used in externally applied drugs in amounts consistent with good manufacturing practice.

(d) *Labeling.* The label of the color additive and any mixtures prepared therefrom intended solely or in part for coloring purposes shall conform to the requirements of § 70.25 of this chapter.

(e) *Certification.* All batches of Ext. D&C Yellow No. 7 shall be certified in accordance with regulations in part 80 of this chapter.

§ 74.1708 D&C Yellow No. 8.

(a) *Identity.* (1) The color additive D&C Yellow No. 8 is principally the disodium salt of fluorescein.

(2) Color additive mixtures for use in externally applied drugs made with D&C Yellow No. 8 may contain only those diluents that are suitable and that are listed in part 73 of this chapter for use in color additive mixtures for coloring externally applied drugs.

(b) *Specifications.* D&C Yellow No. 8 shall be free from impurities other than those named to the extent that

Figure 8

Authorities

8 U.S.C.—Continued	CFR
1446	8 Part 332
1448	8 Parts 310, 312, 322, 324, 337, 339, 341
1452	8 Part 341
1453	8 Part 342
1454—1455	8 Parts 343—343b
1455	8 Part 341
1502	22 Part 50
1503	22 Parts 7, 50
1504	22 Part 50
1522	45 Part 400
1522 note	45 Part 401
1641	8 Part 204
1731—32	8 Part 214
9 U.S.C.	
1—16	10 Part 1023
1629	19 Part 162
10 U.S.C.	
21	32 Part 626
47	32 Part 635
101 et seq	32 Part 158
107	10 Parts 21, 1606
111	32 Part 626
113	32 Parts 10, 12—17, 18, 21, 22, 28, 32—34, 58, 112, 113, 146, 191, 198, 240, 352a, 367, 369, 371, 378, 384, 388, 391, 396, 725
113 note	32 Part 105
121	32 Part 247
125	32 Parts 336, 368, 376, 1280
128	32 Part 223
130	32 Parts 249, 518
131 et seq	32 Parts 18, 355, 358, 363, 365, 373, 377, 385, 387
131	30 Part 376
	31 Part 347
	32 Parts 62b, 187, 205, 234, 346—348, 364, 387
133	32 Parts 70, 73, 142, 145, 211, 247, 262, 337, 338, 370, 374, 382, 384, 390, 392, 395, 765
133a	32 Part 369
136	32 Parts 70, 162, 230, 343, 344, 350, 353, 366, 367a, 380, 383a, 392
137 et seq	48 Part 5433
137	32 Parts 160, 224, 394
	48 Parts 2, 4—6, 8, 9, 11—15, 19, 22, 28, 33, 36, 37, 41, 42, 44, 51, 52
138	32 Part 367
140	32 Parts 10, 12—17, 266
140c	32 Part 250
151—158	32 Part 626
191—193	32 Parts 398, 399
191	32 Parts 371, 381
193	32 Part 362
218	32 Part 516
238	32 Part 510
269	32 Part 44
270	32 Part 101
271—272	32 Part 44
301	32 Parts 153, 341, 342, 386
331 et seq	32 Part 215
331—333	32 Part 501
332—333	32 Part 809a
391	31 Part 210
503—505	32 Part 96

10 U.S.C.—Continued	CFR
503	32 Part 83
503 note	32 Part 316
510—511	32 Part 100
511	32 Part 101
520a	32 Part 96
593	32 Part 100
597	32 Part 100
651	32 Part 100
652	32 Part 44
672—674	32 Part 44
672	32 Part 64
673a	32 Part 101
675	32 Part 64
685	32 Part 44
688	32 Part 64
772	32 Part 53
801 et seq	32 Part 552
801—940	32 Part 143
806	32 Part 776
806a	32 Part 776
814	32 Parts 146, 589, 884
815	32 Part 719
821	32 Part 11
826	32 Part 776
827	32 Part 776
836	32 Part 152
847	32 Part 534
866	32 Part 150
867	32 Part 152
892	32 Part 92
903	32 Part 901
921—932	32 Part 71
939	32 Parts 536, 750, 751, 755—757, 842
	33 Part 25
956	32 Part 765
972	32 Part 45
973	32 Part 64
976	32 Part 143
982	32 Part 144
983	32 Part 216
1005	32 Part 44
1034	33 Part 53
1037	32 Parts 516, 845
1041	32 Part 887
1045	32 Part 78
1054	28 Part 15
1071 et seq	32 Part 799
1071—1093	32 Part 728
1071—1088	32 Part 732
1089	28 Part 15
	32 Parts 61, 516
1091	32 Part 107
1094—1095	32 Part 728
1102	32 Part 518
1121—1122	32 Part 578
1124	19 Part 133
1141 et seq	32 Part 88
1143	32 Part 77
1151	32 Part 254
1161	32 Part 104
1162—1163	32 Part 41
1168	32 Part 45
1171	32 Part 41
1201—1221	32 Part 728
1444	32 Part 48
1475—1480	32 Part 716

775

Figure 9

CHANGES OCTOBER 1, 2004 THROUGH APRIL 29, 2005

TITLE 43 Chapter II—Con.

1610.4–1 Amended 14566
1610.4–2 Revised 14566
1610.4–3 Amended 14566
1610.4–4 Introductory text amended 14566
1610.4–5 Amended 14567
1610.4–6 Amended 14567
1610.4–7 Heading revised; amended 14567
1610.4–8 Amended 14567
1610.4–9 Amended 14567
1610.5–1 Amended 14567
1610.5–3 Amended 14567
1610.5–5 Amended 14567
1610.5–7 Amended 14567
1610.7–1 Amended 14567
1610.8 Amended 14567
1881.10—1881.57 (Subpart 1881) Removed **70562**
2800 Revised 21058
2810 Authority citation revised 21078
2812.1–3 Revised 21078
2880 Revised 21078
2920.6 (b) and (c) amended 21090
9230 Authority citation revised 21090
9239.7–1 Introductory text revised 21090
9260 Authority citation revised 21090
9262.1 Revised 21090

Proposed Rules:

10 .... **61613**
2530 .... **67880**

TITLE 44—EMERGENCY MANAGEMENT AND ASSISTANCE

Chapter I—Federal Emergency Management Agency, Department of Homeland Security (Parts 0—399)

64.6 Tables amended **60310, 61445, 63457, 70378, 75482, 77651**
Tables amended 2818, 6365, 8535, 12601, 16965, 20300, 21160
65.4 Flood elevation determinations; interim **70186, 71718, 72129, 75483**
Flood elevation determinations 2959, 5934, 5936, 9536, 9539
Flood elevation determinations; interim 16730, 16734
67.11 Flood elevation determinations **61446, 70191, 70192, 71722, 72131, 75484**
Flood elevation determinations 5938, 5939, 5942, 9540, 16739
Flood elevation determinations; interim 16736
208 Added; interim 9194

Proposed Rules:

67 .... **61457, 61460, 62013, 63338, 72156, 72158, 75496, 75499**
.... 5949, 5953, 5954, 5956, 10582, 10583, 16786, 16789, 17037, 20326, 20327

TITLE 45—PUBLIC WELFARE

Subtitle A—Department of Health and Human Services (Parts 1—199)

144 Authority citation revised **78780**
144.103 Revised **78780**
146 Authority citation revised **78783**
146.111 Revised **78783**
146.113 Revised **78788**
146.115 Revised **78788**
146.117 Revised **78794**
146.119 Revised **78797**
146.125 Revised **78797**
Correctly amended 21147
146.143 Revised **78797**
(b), (c)(2)(i), (ii) and (iii) correctly amended 21147
146.145 Revised **78797**

Chapter III—Office of Child Support Enforcement (Child Support Enforcement Program), Administration for Children and Families, Department of Health and Human Services (Parts 300—399)

303.8 (c) amended; interim **77661**
303.72 (b)(1), (2) introductory text, (d)(1), (2), (f)(3), (g)(4) and (i)(1) revised **62415**

Chapter XVI—Legal Services Corporation (Parts 1600—1699)

1611 Appendix A revised 10327

NOTE: **Boldface page numbers indicate 2004 changes.**

Figure 10

APRIL 2005 **73**

CHANGES OCTOBER 1, 2004 THROUGH APRIL 29, 2005

Chapter XXV—Corporation for National and Community Service (Parts 2500—2599)

2551.12 (r) and (w) revised **60094**
2551.21 Revised **60095**
2551.23 (c)(1) revised **60095**
2551.121 (g) redesignated as (g)(1); (g)(2) added **60095**
2552.12 (u) and (z) revised **60095**
2552.21 Revised **60095**
2552.23 (c)(1) revised **60095**
2552.121 (g) redesignated as (g)(1); (g)(2) added **60095**
2553.12 (o) and (r) revised **60095**
2553.21 Revised **60095**
2553.23 (c)(1) revised **60095**
2553.91 (g) redesignated as (g)(1); (g)(2) added **60095**

Proposed Rules:

98 .... **64881**
146 .... **78800, 78825**
160 20224
164 20224
650 .... **71395**
1356 4803
1801 .... 3178, 12436
2500—2599 (Ch. XXV) **60603**

TITLE 46—SHIPPING

Chapter I—Coast Guard, Department of Homeland Security (Parts 1—199)

10.805 (f) amended **68089**
12.02-3 (b)(3) revised **68089**
12.15-5 (c) amended **68089**
28.30 (a) amended **68089**
30.15-1 (a) amended **68089**
30.30-11 (b) amended **68089**
115.620 Second section correctly removed; CFR correction 20302

Chapter II—Maritime Administration, Department of Transportation (Parts 200—399)

232.2 (d) revised **61449**
232.6 (a) and (b) revised **61449**
281.1 (f) revised **61449**
287.4 (a) revised **61451**
295.11 (b) introductory text revised **61451**
295.23 Introductory text revised **61451**
298.3 (a)(1) revised **61451**
298.13 (c)(2) introductory text revised **61451**
310.7 (b)(6) revised; interim **61606**
310.57 (a) revised **61451**
310.58 (d) revised **61454**
Regulation at 69 FR 29081 confirmed **74455**
355.1 (b) and (c) revised **61451**
380.22 (b) and (c) revised **61452**
380.23 Revised **61452**
390.2 (a)(1) revised **61452**

Chapter III—Coast Guard (Great Lakes Pilotage), Department of Homeland Security (Parts 400—499)

401 Technical correction 13574, 15779
401.405 (a) and (b) revised; interim 12103
401.407 (a) and (b) revised; interim 12103
401.410 A, B and (c) revised; interim 12103
401.420 (a), (b), (c)(1) and (3) amended; interim 12104
401.428 Amended; interim 12104

Chapter IV—Federal Maritime Commission (Parts 500—599)

501 Revised 7659
501.26 (c) and (d) revised; (o) and (p) added **64414**
502.51 (a) amended 10329
502.62 (g) revised 10329
502.68 (a)(3) revised 10329
502.69 (b) revised 10329
502.182 Amended 10329
502.271 (f)(1) amended 7669
(d)(5) revised 10329
502.304 (b) amended 10329
502.401 Amended 7669
503.43 (c)(i), (ii), (3)(ii), (iii), (4), (d) and (e) revised; (c)(2) amended 10329
503.69 (b)(2) revised 10330
515.5 (a) amended 7669
(a), (b)(1), (2) and (3) revised 10330
515.12 (a) amended 7669
515.18 (a) amended 7669
515.22 (e) amended 7669
515.25 (a) amended 7669

NOTE: Boldface page numbers indicate 2004 changes.

Figure 11

CHAPTER 1

GENERAL FIRE PREVENTION REGULATIONS

SECTION:

8-1-1: **ADOPTION OF FIRE CODE:**

A. Code Adopted By Reference: The international fire code, 2003 edition, is hereby adopted by reference except for such provisions as are specifically hereinafter deleted, modified or amended.

B. Compliance With Chapter: Every existing building, structure or part thereof shall comply with the requirements of this chapter.

C. Copy On File: One copy of the international fire code, including all amendments made in this section shall be kept on file in the office of the city clerk.

D. Amendments: The following sections are hereby amended from the international fire code, 2003 edition, adopted in subsection A of this section:

Chapter 1 Administration: Section 101.1 Title Insert: City of Carbondale.
(Ord. 2003-75)

8-1-2: **BUILDINGS TO CONFORM TO FIRE CODE:** No wall, structure, building, or part thereof, shall hereafter be built, enlarged, or altered, until a sketch of the work, together with a statement of the materials to be used, shall have been submitted in duplicate to the building and neighborhood services manager for inspection and investigation to see if same be found to be in accordance with the provisions of the

ATTORNEY GENERAL OPINIONS

This section refers specifically to those *attorney general* (AG) opinions of the individual states. The *attorney general* is generally the highest ranking lawyer for the state government. Aside from prosecuting certain crimes and enforcing or defending the state government's rights (if you sue your state for wrongful condemnation of your property, the AG's office will handle the case on behalf of the state), the attorney general's office will give *advisory opinions.*

Advisory opinions, providing interpretations of law by the attorney general's office, are given upon request of the state governor, state agencies, lawyers, or in some cases, private individuals, who require an interpretation of law. This is considered necessary when there are no court cases construing a particular statute, or when the cases construing a law are either contradictory or do not address the exact nature of the problem. In some states, such opinions are considered binding law in the absence of a court opinion to the contrary.

Attorney general opinions are usually issued in slip form, although most states do eventually bind them. Indexing is commonly done either quarterly, semiannually, or annually.

EXECUTIVE ORDERS AND PROCLAMATIONS

The President of the United States has the authority to issue *executive orders*, which are typically directed to other government officials in order to manage the operations of the federal government, and *proclamations*, which are usually announcements or policy statements. For example, on October 8, 2001, President George W. Bush signed Executive Order 13228, which created the Office of Homeland Security and the Homeland Security Council. On April 29, 2005, President Bush proclaimed May 1, 2005, "Law Day, USA." Both executive orders and proclamations are issued and numbered sequentially.

You may, on occasion, need to read the text of an executive order or proclamation. They are published in a number of sources, including:

- *Federal Register* (Daily);
- *United States Code Congressional and Administrative News* (USCCAN);
- *United States Code Service Advance* (USCSA);
- *Weekly Compilation of Presidential Documents* (which are then compiled in the *Public Papers of the Presidents*); and,
- Title 3 of the *Code of Federal Regulations* (C.F.R.).

You can find executive orders and proclamations on the National Archive's Federal Register website, at **www.archives.gov/federal-register/executive-orders/index.html**, or via GPO Access's Federal Register page, at **www.gpoaccess.gov/fr/index.html**. Executive orders and proclamations from the current U.S. President can be accessed via the White House website, **www.whitehouse.gov**.

LOCAL ORDINANCES

In addition to being subject to federal and state laws, you may also be affected by local laws or ordinances, which can cover everything from car radio noise restrictions and other traffic regulations to whether you can operate a business in your home. Ordinances can be passed by towns, cities, counties, or other forms of local government, and are sometimes called *municipal ordinances*. Ordinances initially are passed in the form of slip laws (each ordinance is published separately and is unbound), but many jurisdictions eventually *codify* (group by subject) the ordinances so they are easier to locate and research. (see Figure 11, p.66.) While you can generally find either copies of ordinances or local ordinance codes at your town or city hall, county courthouse, or other local government administrative office, also check out your local public or academic library. In addition, many local government websites include full-text versions of ordinances or codes (many are also keyword searchable).

A number of online ordinance publishers and directories provide links to municipal ordinances.

- *Municode.com*—**www.municode.com/index.asp**
- *LexisNexis Municipal Codes*—**municipalcodes.lexisnexis.com**
- *E-Codes Municipal Codes on the Internet*—**www.generalcode.com/webcode2.html**
- *American Legal Publishing's Code Library*—**www.amlegal.com/library**
- *Sterling Codifiers' Codes Online*—**66.113.195.234/online.html**

BAR ASSOCIATIONS

Another source of potentially helpful legal information is a *bar association*. Bar associations are professional organizations of lawyers that provide services to its members and may offer legal information and other forms of assistance to the general public, such as lawyer referral directories and pro bono assistance. Bar Associations may publish bar journals (which often publish articles on very practical oriented legal subjects) and issue legal ethics opinions (advisory statements about what constitutes appropriate lawyer conduct).

There are many types of bar associations, including national (e.g., American Bar Association); state (e.g., Illinois State Bar Association); local, court, or regional (e.g., Jackson County Bar Association, Bar Association of the Central and Southern Federal Districts of Illinois, etc.); and subject (e.g., Illinois Trial Lawyers Association, California Women Lawyers, etc.). To find your state or local bar association, check your phone book for local listings (often listed under lawyer referral), or consult one of the following online directories.

- American Bar Association, State and Local Bar Association Directory—**www.abanet.org/barserv/stlobar.html**

- Resources for Attorneys, State or Local Bar Associations—**www.resourcesforattorneys.com/barassociations.html**

- Heiros Gamos, North America Bar Associations—**www.hg.org/northam-bar.html**

Researching Case Law

chapter 4

If your question has not been answered or your problem has not been solved, you will need to research actual case law.

CASE LAW DEFINED

Case law refers to the written opinions of judges in specific lawsuits. These opinions, or court decisions, are published in books called *reporters*. Generally, the only opinions that are published in reporters are appellate *court decisions*. This means that a case will not have an opinion printed in a reporter if the case only went as far as the trial court, but very often, the trial court decision will not even be written.

All cases, both civil and criminal, begin in a *trial court,* or the court where the facts and legal issues are first determined during a lawsuit. In the trial court, the case may end in a *plea bargain* or negotiation between a prosecutor and a defendant, allowing a defendant to plead guilty and receive a lesser punishment (in a criminal case). It could end in *settlement* when parties to a lawsuit come to an agreement. It could end in *dismissal* without trial, meaning that the judge discharges the lawsuit, or a trial may be held with or without a jury. The trial court is known by many names, depending on the state or jurisdiction, what area of law is involved, and how much money is involved.

See Figure 12 on page 87 for a diagram of the state and federal court systems. The federal system is fairly simple, but the state system can become a bit more complicated. As you can see from Figure 12, names for state courts (especially state trial courts) can vary greatly. Examples are given for some of the states that use each of the various titles. This is not a complete listing, and some states use more than one title, depending on the type of case involved or even the county where the court is located. For example, in Virginia, depending upon the location of the court, divorce cases may be heard in either circuit court, domestic relations court, or experimental family court. Other states may have subdivisions, such as *circuit court, probate division*.

In many states there are actually two levels of trial court, depending upon the amount of money in dispute or the type of case. For example, Michigan has district courts, which primarily handle civil cases involving less than $25,000 and criminal misdemeanor cases. Civil cases involving more than $25,000 or criminal felonies are handled in the circuit courts. Furthermore, some cases in the district courts may be appealed to the circuit court. Therefore, the circuit court acts mostly as a trial court, but occasionally as an appellate court. To further complicate matters, some state court cases may also be appealed to the federal court.

If one party does not agree with the trial court's decision (or even a settlement reached without a trial), he or she may appeal it to a higher court, called an *appellate court*. These decisions are usually written and are published. You should know that most cases are not appealed. Many people do not want to spend the money on an appeal, which can be quite costly as well as time-consuming, or they may feel that they do not have a clearly appealable issue. Because of these reasons, many cases are not printed.

Precedent

Only reported cases have weight in the legal system because case law sets *precedent*. Precedent means that the court's opinion furnishes an example, or *authority*, for an identical or similar case based on a similar question of law. Precedent can help you select a course of action for your situation. If there is precedent for your circumstances, your position will be strengthened.

You will want to find the most recent case displaying the precedent for your particular problem. For example, if you find a case from 1958 supporting your position, but a 1989 case contradicts your position, you have an obstacle you must overcome. Conversely, if the 1989 opinion supports your position, you will be in a strong position.

If you find a case that is identical to yours in every way, the case is said to be *on all fours* or *on point*. This is the best kind of case you could find in researching, but unfortunately, cases that mirror yours are hard to find. You will likely find more cases that are only marginally on point. They may have some elements that are the same as your problem and a few that are similar, while the rest of the case is not related. These cases may still be useful, especially if you can show that the situations are similar and draw analogies.

You will find many more cases that, while the area of law is identical, the situations are totally different. Do not try to compare apples and oranges if you find such cases. Remember them if they describe the area of law well, but otherwise, you will be better off looking for cases with more similarities.

One other consideration must be given to the cases you find in your research. This is whether the case is *binding precedent* or *persuasive precedent*. Binding precedent means that the court *must* follow it. Usually, each trial court is under a certain appellate court. The decisions of that appellate court must be followed by the trial court.

Example:

Suppose your case is in a federal district court in Florida. The federal district courts in Florida are under the U.S. Court of Appeals for the Eleventh Circuit, which also covers Alabama and Georgia. If the case you found is from the Eleventh Circuit, it is binding precedent that must be followed by the federal district court in Florida. On the other hand, if the case you found is from the U.S. Court of Appeals for the Second

Circuit (which covers Connecticut, New York, and Vermont), it is not binding on the Florida federal district court.

If the case is not binding, it is only *persuasive precedent*. That is, you can use it to argue that it is a good way to view the law, but the court will not be required to follow it. Therefore, it is best to look for cases from your state or your federal appeals circuit.

DIGESTS

Digests are the primary printed source for finding case law in reporters (described on page 78 in the section titled "Case Reporters"). This is because case opinions are not typically published in reporters by subject, and individual reporters only contain an index for cases reported in each individual reporter. The digest is a compilation of *abstracts*, or summaries, of cases in a particular jurisdiction or legal area. These abstracts, along with the topic and key number (discussed in the subsection on page 76 titled "Topic and Key Number"), are an integral part of the way legal research is conducted. When these abstracts are printed in a reporter, they are called *headnotes*, which is discussed fully in the section on reporters.

State, Federal, or Decennial

Each jurisdiction, whether state or federal, has its own digest. There is one digest for New York, one for Texas, one for California, a combined digest for Virginia and West Virginia, and so on. Each digest is approximately thirty or forty volumes, with the exception of the decennial digests, which have substantially more volumes than either the individual state digests or the federal digests. Digests may also have more than one edition, so be sure to use the latest edition.

Example:

You would want to use *Florida Digest 2d* before looking in *Florida Digest*, since *Florida Digest* covers cases decided before 1935. You should always search for the newest possible cases.

Decennial digests (*decennials*) are sets of digests that cover all of the states and all federal jurisdictions as well. They are grouped in ten-year periods, hence the name *decennial*. Since the *9th Decennial Digest*, the decennials have grown at such a tremendous rate that each ten-year period has been broken down into two five-year periods, for example, *11th Decennial Digest, Part I*.

Just to give you an idea of the growth rate, which corresponds directly to the number of cases being heard at the appellate level, the following is the breakdown of the number of volumes in the 7th, 8th, 9th, 10th, and 11th decennial:

7th Decennial Digest:	38 volumes
8th Decennial Digest:	50 volumes
9th Decennial Digest (Parts 1 & 2):	108 volumes
10th Decennial Digest (Parts 1 & 2):	64 volumes
11th Decennial Digest (Parts 1 & 2):	up to volume 45 in 2005

If you research in the decennials, you treat each ten-year period as if it were a separate set of books, unless you are researching in the 9th, 10th, or 11th decennials, where you would research each part separately. Additionally, the decennials are updated by a set of books called the *General Digest*, which is in the 11th series. Each individual volume of this set must be researched individually until a compilation index is published. The compilation is in the back of each tenth volume (10th, 20th, 30th, etc.).

You are probably wondering why anyone would want to search through the decennials since they appear to be so cumbersome. Unless you plan on doing an all-encompassing search of all jurisdictions, you can avoid researching in the decennials. Any cases you would find in them can also be found in the individual state or federal digests, so they are usually used as a last effort.

Before beginning any search in a digest, you will benefit from browsing through a few volumes to see the layout of the books.

Accessing the Digest System

You access the digests through an index, generally called the *Descriptive Word Index*. (see Figure 13 on page 88.) Follow the directions for using an index in Chapter 1. Remember to look up every possible relevant word or phrase you can think of. Do not get discouraged if you do not find any of them at first. Continue to think of different words or phrases until you find a listing. Remember to use the dictionary, thesaurus, and *Words and Phrases*. When you find a listing that pertains to your topic, write down the information.

Topic and Key Number

You will find that a digest index does not refer you to a page. Instead, it refers you to a word, phrase, or abbreviation in boldfaced type, and a number; for example, "**Divorce 238**." This is called a *topic and key number*. There is a table in the front of each digest volume listing what each topic abbreviation represents. For example, *Evid* is an abbreviation for *Evidence*, and *App & E* is an abbreviation for *Appeal and Error*.

The main volumes of the digest are set up alphabetically, like a standard encyclopedia, but instead of saying "Photography to Pumpkin," it will likely say "Pretrial Procedure to Records." When you go to the volume containing "Divorce," turn the pages until you see "Divorce," followed by the picture of a key and the number "238" in the upper right or upper left hand corner. It is this "Divorce 238" that is the topic and key number, "Divorce" being the topic and "238" being the key number. (see Figure 14 on page 89.)

Notice that the page is double-columned and is filled with small paragraphs. These paragraphs are abstracts, or summaries, of all the cases in that jurisdiction discussing that distinct point of law. Only that one element of the law will be considered under "Divorce 238," in this case the nature and right of permanent alimony. A different element of the law will be discussed under "Divorce 239." The digest system reduces each and every point to its own topic and key number.

NOTE: *When you discover a useful topic and key number in one jurisdiction, you can look up cases in any other jurisdiction as well. Digests using the key number system are published by one publisher, West Publishing Company, and the topic and key number system is uniform throughout the entire digest system.*

If you proceed to "Divorce 238" in another digest, you will notice that those case abstracts, although dealing with another state or court, discuss the exact same point of law.

Example:
Assume you have been researching Florida law and "Divorce 238," *permanent alimony*, is pertinent to your research. You decide you would like to see New York cases dealing with permanent alimony. All you need to do is look up "Divorce 238" in the digest for New York. The topic will be the same. Try it with Hawaii, Michigan, Texas, or any other state. You will see that the subject matter of "Divorce 238" is the same for each of those states as well.

Reading a Case Citation

Each case summary from the digest will give you the complete *citation* of the case to which it refers. A citation is the way all legal materials are quoted. It is a form of legal shorthand used to give information about where a case or statute can be found. When you have a citation, you will already know a great deal of information about a case. A case citation looks like the following example.

> *Roth Greeting Cards v. United Card Co.*, 429 F.2d 1106 (9th Cir. 1970).

"Roth Greeting Cards v. United Card Co." means Roth Greeting Cards versus United Card Co., in which Roth Greeting Cards is the party that brought the appeal (having lost in the trial court) and United Card Co. is the party defending against the appeal (having won in the trial court). The first-named party is always the party appealing the case.

The number "429" refers to volume 429. "F.2d" is an abbreviation of the reporter, in this instance, Federal Reporter, 2nd Series. "1106" refers to page 1106, and "1970" refers to the year the case was decided.

Sometimes a case citation will give additional information as well, such as the abbreviation of the court that wrote the opinion, in this case, the 9th Circuit Court of Appeals.

If the case summary seems relevant to your problem, write down the citation. Then you can look the case up in the reporter and read the full text of the opinion.

– Warning –

Never argue a point of law based on a case abstract from a digest, statute annotation, or elsewhere. You must read the full text of the opinion to determine if the case really applies to your problem.

Pocket Parts

Now is a good time to discuss *pocket parts*. A pocket part is a small pamphlet placed in a slat or pocket in the book. Usually, the pocket is placed on the inside back cover, but is occasionally on the inside front cover. The pocket part is a supplement or update of the hardbound volume. Publishers use pocket parts to avoid reprinting the volume with each change in the law, which occurs frequently. It is essential to always look in the pocket part for new information if a set of books is updated with pocket parts. The information in the pocket part will be laid out in the identical manner to the main volume it is supplementing. Although not all books are updated in this manner, digests are, so if you are researching "Divorce 238," you can look it up in the pocket part exactly as you did in the main volume.

CASE REPORTERS

As stated earlier, *case reporters* are sets of books in which court opinions are printed.

Opinions

A *court opinion* is the written decision of a court. Although the word "opinion" is used, do not confuse it with its common meaning. A court's opinion is much more than the judge's belief about a legal matter. A court's opinion is a formal statement explaining how the court applied the law to a particular set of circumstances to arrive at its determination of the case. It is *binding* on the parties concerned; that is, all parties involved in the case *must* comply with the court's decision or be subject to contempt of court. *Contempt of court*, meaning that a judge believes that a participant in his or her courtroom was willfully disobedient or disrespectful to the judge, the court itself, or the law, could include a monetary fine or jail.

As said before, in general, only appellate court decisions are reported. (There are exceptions, which are discussed on page 82 under the subheading "Federal Cases.") Appellate court cases are customarily heard by a panel—a group of judges that is smaller than the entire court. For example, if an appellate court has nine judges total, it will probably be split into three panels of three judges each. This means that if a panel hears an appellate argument, three judges will listen to the argument. On occasion however, the full court may sit and provide an opinion.

The Supreme Court of the United States is an appellate court in which all nine justices sit and listen to arguments. When all of an appellate court's judges sit in on an argument it is called *en banc,* which means *in the bench* or *full bench. Argument* refers to the remarks or oral presentation made in court by attorneys on behalf of the parties involved.

Parts of an opinion. A court's opinion may consist of up to three *parts*—the majority, the dissent, and the concurrence.

The majority opinion. The *majority opinion* of an appellate court decision is one in which the majority of the court's members have joined and agreed. It is usually written by one judge, and the other judges declare that they agree with his or her opinion. This means that if the panel listening to the argument has three judges, at least two judges must agree with each other for there to be a majority opinion. If nine judges are sitting on the panel, at least five must agree with each other for the opinion to be the majority opinion. The majority opinion is the opinion that the parties to the lawsuit must abide by. This is also the opinion that you will look to as precedent when you do research.

The dissent. The *dissent* (or *dissenting* or *minority opinion*) is a separate opinion, in which one or more judges of a court expressly disagree with the majority. Often, the judge or judges disagreeing with the majority will write an individual opinion explaining why he or she disagrees, although a judge may dissent without writing an explanation. The dissenting opinion does not set precedent.

NOTE: *If you discover while doing your research that all you can find are cases that only have support for your position in the dissent or concurrence, you will have to try to make a persuasive argu-*

ment. It will not have the same weight that the precedent set in the majority opinion has, and in fact, will probably be ignored by most judges. This is usually an indication that your position is not very good.

The concurrence. In a *concurrence*, or *concurring opinion*, a judge (or judges) agrees with the conclusion of the majority, but disagrees with the reasoning.

Example:
The majority opinion says that Smith shall recover money for injuries he received in a car accident with Jones, and sets out all the legal rules and principles it followed to come to that conclusion. By concurring, a judge is saying, "I agree that Smith should recover the money for his injuries, but for different reasons than those legal rules and principles followed by the majority." Perhaps the majority states that Smith should prevail based on the theory of negligence, while the concurring judge thinks that he should prevail because of the theory of strict liability.

It is possible for the entire panel to disagree as to the legal rules and principles followed to come to a conclusion. All, or most, of the judges may write concurring opinions. When this happens, the opinion is not called a majority, since no consensus of the court has been reached. It is called a *plurality* instead.

In our previous example, Smith would still recover money for his injuries, since the panel would agree to that result, but no clear precedent explaining why he prevailed would be set, since the judges could not agree as to the legal reasons why Smith should recover the money. Always look for a case in which clear precedent has been set.

Per Curiam Opinion

A *per curiam opinion* is not a part of an opinion, but a type of opinion. Meaning *by the court*, it is one in which the entire court joins, but the name of the judge who wrote the opinion is not revealed, and as a rule, the opinion will state a result without giving a reason. Consequently, per curiam opinions are not given great weight.

THE REPORTER SYSTEM

The *reporter system* is a collection of opinions that are published in sets. Each volume of the set is numbered consecutively and each case in the volume is printed chronologically.

State Cases

Most reporters are published by West Publishing Company. West publishes the cases in *regional reporters*, which divide the country into regions. The regional reporters and the states they cover are displayed in Table 1 on page 92.

Most jurisdictions also have their own reporters. There are two types of these reporters—*official* and *unofficial*. It will suffice for you to know that official reporters are published by the state itself and the unofficial reporters are generally published by West Publishing Company. Most states have discontinued publication of official reporters because it costs too much to publish and West does a good job of reporting. Whether you read a case in an official or an unofficial reporter is not important to your research. The case will read the same except for any editorial comment that West Publishing, or other reporting service, will prepare before the case. Also, because of the prohibitive cost of upkeep, most libraries do not stock the official reporters of other states.

NOTE: *When you look up a case in, for example,* ***Florida Cases*** *(this is a special version of the* ***Southern Reporter, 2d Series*** *that only includes cases from Florida courts), you may notice that the book skips between pages 5 and 60 or between pages 131 and 164—in other words, the pages may not be consecutive. If you had looked up your case in the regional reporter,* ***Southern Reporter, 2d Series****, however, those pages would have been there. That is because pages 6 through 59 covered cases from another state that were published in that region. There is no need to be nervous and think that the book is defective or that someone tore pages from the book.*

Federal Cases

Publication of reporters for the federal system is a little easier to remember than the state reporter system because there are no regional reporters in the federal system. All *Federal Reporters* correspond to the court from which the cases come, regardless of their geographical area.

Example:
A Court of Appeals case from Pennsylvania will be reported in Federal Reporter, as will a Court of Appeals case from California.

The federal system, which is separated into *circuits*, is described in Table 2 on page 93.

In general, there are only seven sets of reporters in the federal reporter system. All courts of appeal cases are published in the Federal Reporter, as stated above. All bankruptcy court cases are published in *Bankruptcy Reporter*, and certain federal cases concerning rules of procedure and evidence may be published in *Federal Rules Decisions*.

Although trial (i.e., district court) cases are not usually published, a few are printed in the *Federal Supplement*. This is the exception to the general rule that only appellate cases are reported. The judge who hears the case determines if the case will be published, and in general, only 1–10% of federal district court cases are printed.

Federal Court of Appeals cases that do not appear in the printed Federal Reporter (i.e., opinions that are either unpublished or not cleared by the court for *official publication*) are printed in a reporter called *Federal Appendix*, which began in 2001. Although you can read the case opinions and may use their legal reasoning, many jurisdictions will not allow you to cite to these *unpublished opinions*.

Cases that predate 1880 are printed in *Federal Cases*. With the exception of Federal Cases, which compiles cases reported from 1789–1879 and is arranged alphabetically, all reporters are compiled chronologically, like the state reporters. All of these sets of books are published by West Publishing Company.

United States Supreme Court cases are published in three separate reporters, published by three different publishers. All Supreme Court cases will be found in each set of books.

The first is an official reporter published by the United States Government Printing Office (GPO). In it, cases are printed without any editorial comment. This set of books is usually six to nine months behind in publication. It is called *United States Reports* (U.S.).

The second is published by West Publishing and is called *Supreme Court Reporter* (S.Ct.). The editorial commentary is identical to that of every other reporter in the West reporter system, which, as you can see by now, encompasses most of the reporters—state and federal. This editorial commentary will be described in full detail on page 84.

The third set of books that compiles the United States Supreme Court decisions is *United States Reports, Lawyers Edition* (L.Ed. or L.Ed. 2d). This should not be confused with the *United States Reports* published by the GPO. In addition to any commentary before the actual case is reported, *Lawyers Edition* has the *briefs* (a written outline of the attorneys' arguments) written by the attorneys, and any *amicus curae* (which means *friends of the court*) in a section in the back of each volume. The briefs may help you see how legal arguments are made to a court.

Headnotes

One of the most important aspects of a case in the West system is the *headnote*, which was briefly discussed in the section on digests on page 28. Headnotes precede the actual printed opinion in the reporter. A *headnote* is a brief summary of a legal rule or significant fact in a case. In a digest, this would be the abstract of a case. The headnote is important to legal research, because once you find a headnote that is important, you can go back to the digest and find additional cases covering that topic.

Study Figure 15 on pages 90 and 91, which is a copy of the first two pages of a case reported in volume 658 of the *Pacific Reporter, 2d Series*. Notice that after the *syllabus*, or summary of the case, there are a series of numbers, 1 through 10, followed by topics and key numbers, and then case abstracts. The numbers, 1–10, and the abstracts are called the headnotes. (Technically, the topic and key number are not part of the headnote; however, most people consider the entire paragraph to be the headnote.)

Now, assume that you find this case in the digest for Alaska when you determine that the topic and key number *Indians 24* may be important to your research. As you glance at the headnotes, however, you notice that *Indians 27(1)* is also very important. You can return to the digest, look up "Indians 27(1)," and find additional cases related to your problem. Remember, just as you cannot use the digest abstracts as the sole basis for your research, you cannot use headnotes in that fashion. Unless the headnote is taken verbatim from the text of the opinion, you may never quote a headnote in any court document.

Another interesting editorial aspect of headnotes is that the number of the headnote makes it easy to find that point of law or fact in the case itself. You may have a case that is ten, twenty, or even fifty pages long. What if only headnote 5 applies to your problem? How would you find that point of law without reading through the entire case? Notice in Figure 15 that immediately after "II. DISCUSSION" there is a "[1]." This bracketed number refers to headnote number 1. The point of law or facts corresponding to headnote 1 will be discussed in that section of the opinion. This is an especially handy tool when your case is long and has many headnotes. (Headnotes are also helpful when you are using *Shepard's Citations*, discussed in detail in Chapter 5.)

Other Editorial Comment

The *syllabus* is a summary of the case being reported. This syllabus is not part of the case, and neither are the headnotes. This is because neither the syllabus nor the headnotes were written by the court. These were added by the publisher to help you save time in your research. Look at Figure 15 once more. After headnote number 10, there is a short horizontal line. All the material *after* that line is the actual case opinion and may be quoted as legally significant, since it was written by the court.

Incidentally, the citation for the case shown in Figure 15 is, *Native Village of Eyak v. GC Contractors*, 658 P.2d 756 (Alaska 1983).

Advance Sheets

Not all sets of legal books are updated with pocket parts. Case reporters are numbered consecutively and the opinions are printed in chronological order. Any supplementation required must *follow* the last case in the set. For this reason, reporters are updated by use of *advance sheets* that add new case opinions to the set, instead of with pocket parts, which supplement existing materials. Advance sheets are not really sheets (as in separate sheets of paper), but are pamphlets. Unlike pocket parts, they have a cover and are placed at the end of the last volume in the set of reporters instead of being placed inside the volumes. The cases are laid out exactly as they are in the hardbound reporter volumes.

There may be as many as twenty advance sheets on the library shelf for each set of reporters, but that should not worry you. Each advance sheet is numbered in a fashion corresponding to the reporter series, so when a suitable number of cases have been printed in the advance sheets, the publisher will print a hardbound edition, and the advance sheets for that volume will be discarded. For example, if the last hardbound volume in the reporter series *Pacific Reporter, 3rd Series* (P.3d) is number 32, pages 1–183 of Volume 33 will be printed as advance sheets until there are enough pamphlets to print a hardbound Volume 33. When a hardbound Volume 33 is released, the advance sheets corresponding to Volume 33 will be discarded.

Looseleaf Services

Looseleaf services, sometimes just called *looseleafs*, are just what the name suggests—looseleaf binders. These sets of books may be one volume but are usually multiple volumes. Looseleafs are used for many different types of legal materials, but case reporting is one of their major uses. Looseleaf services are always published by private companies.

The main advantage of looseleaf services, and the reason many legal practitioners use them and buy subscriptions, is that looseleaf publishers print new cases and other legal materials much faster than the materials printed in reporters. Since the materials are just inserted into looseleaf binders, they do not require binding, which can extend printing time significantly.

Up until just five or six years ago, the time difference between the first printing in a looseleaf and the printing in a reporter advance sheet could have been three to four weeks or more. Today, the lag is not as acute for those with access to computerized databases (see Chapter 7), but it is still at least two weeks without computer access. This time difference could be very important in some instances, especially when a new case affects the potential outcome of a client's problem.

Occasionally, there are cases that are not even printed in a reporter. Some looseleaf services print these cases.

Looseleafs are generally easy to use. They are updated either by inserting new materials behind previously printed ones, or by removing old pages and inserting new ones in their place. This is a tedious process that does not affect the user, since it is done by the library staff. Only cite a case in a looseleaf if you cannot find it in a reporter, either because it is not printed in a reporter yet or it is the type of case that is not printed in a reporter at all.

Figure 12

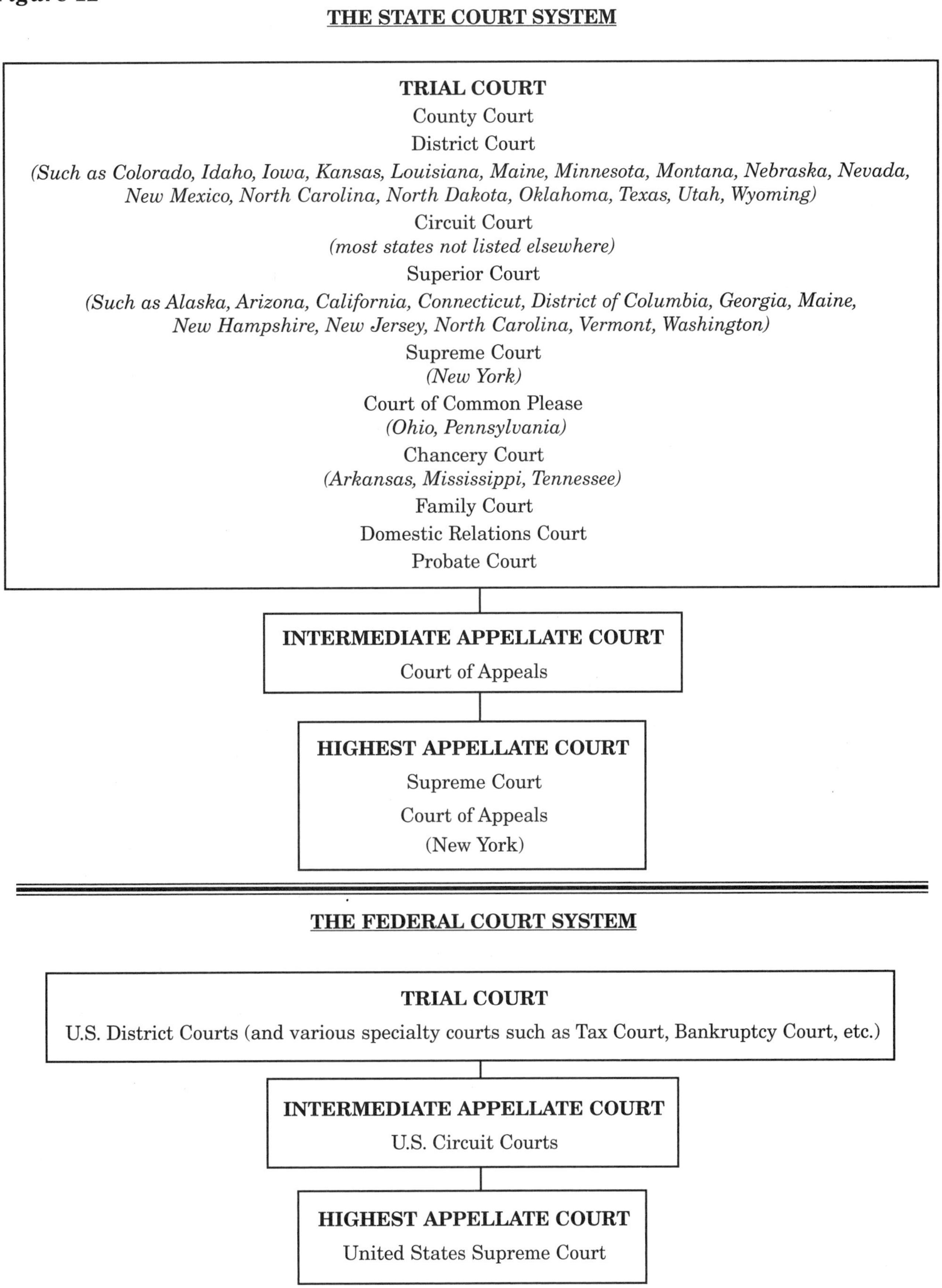

THE STATE COURT SYSTEM

TRIAL COURT
County Court
District Court
(Such as Colorado, Idaho, Iowa, Kansas, Louisiana, Maine, Minnesota, Montana, Nebraska, Nevada, New Mexico, North Carolina, North Dakota, Oklahoma, Texas, Utah, Wyoming)
Circuit Court
(most states not listed elsewhere)
Superior Court
(Such as Alaska, Arizona, California, Connecticut, District of Columbia, Georgia, Maine, New Hampshire, New Jersey, North Carolina, Vermont, Washington)
Supreme Court
(New York)
Court of Common Please
(Ohio, Pennsylvania)
Chancery Court
(Arkansas, Mississippi, Tennessee)
Family Court
Domestic Relations Court
Probate Court

INTERMEDIATE APPELLATE COURT
Court of Appeals

HIGHEST APPELLATE COURT
Supreme Court
Court of Appeals
(New York)

THE FEDERAL COURT SYSTEM

TRIAL COURT
U.S. District Courts (and various specialty courts such as Tax Court, Bankruptcy Court, etc.)

INTERMEDIATE APPELLATE COURT
U.S. Circuit Courts

HIGHEST APPELLATE COURT
United States Supreme Court

Figure 13

63 Ill D 2d-119

ALIMONY

References are to Digest Topics and Key Numbers

Figure 14

should have allowed wife one-half of the $400 and reasonable solicitor's fees and alimony.

Goodman v. Goodman, 26 N.E.2d 631, 304 Ill.App. 587.

⚷238. —— **Defenses and objections.**

Ill. 1940. Generally, when divorce is awarded husband on wife's fault, wife will not be awarded permanent alimony. S.H.A. ch. 40, § 19.

Adler v. Adler, 26 N.E.2d 504, 373 Ill. 361, certiorari denied 61 S.Ct. 29, 311 U.S. 670, 85 L.Ed. 430.

Ill.App. 1 Dist. 1993. Trial court acted within its discretion by barring wife from seeking maintenance as part of judgment of dissolution, where property allotted to wife, including her share of retirement funds, was valued well in excess of $1 million.

In re Marriage of Andrew, 194 Ill.Dec. 724, 628 N.E.2d 221, 258 Ill.App.3d 924.

Ill.App. 1 Dist. 1992. Award of maintenance to wife in dissolution proceeding was within trial court's discretion, despite lack of any indication that wife intended to change her position or further her education. S.H.A. ch. 40, ¶ 504.

In re Marriage of Maczko, 201 Ill.Dec. 127, 636 N.E.2d 559, 263 Ill.App.3d 991.

Ill.App. 1 Dist. 1992. In determining ability to meet one's needs, party seeking maintenance is not required to liquidate assets or impair capital in order to maintain standard of living established during marriage. S.H.A. ch. 40, ¶ 504(b).

In re Marriage of Pearson, 177 Ill.Dec. 650, 603 N.E.2d 720, 236 Ill.App.3d 337.

Ill.App. 1 Dist. 1992. Post-marital support should be accomplished through just distribution of marital assets whenever possible, rather than maintenance. S.H.A. ch. 40, ¶¶ 504(a), 504 note.

Flynn v. Flynn, 173 Ill.Dec. 735, 597 N.E.2d 709, 232 Ill.App.3d 394, appeal denied 176 Ill.Dec. 797, 602 N.E.2d 451, 146 Ill.2d 626.

Ill.App. 1 Dist. 1991. Spouse receiving maintenance need not consume his or her share of marital property to be entitled to maintenance. S.H.A. ch. 40, ¶ 504(a).

In re Marriage of Kennedy, 158 Ill.Dec. 172, 573 N.E.2d 1357, 214 Ill.App.3d 849.

Ill.App. 1 Dist. 1991. Court may deny maintenance when assets awarded to party generate sufficient income to meet her needs. S.H.A. ch. 40, ¶ 504(b).

In re Marriage of Malinowski, 156 Ill.Dec. 3, 570 N.E.2d 479, 211 Ill.App.3d 536.

Ill.App. 1 Dist. 1991. Former wife, who was 65 years old and had not worked outside the home for 40 years, was entitled to permanent maintenance; wife was not required to sell assets or impair her capital in order to generate income from which she could support herself in manner enjoyed during marriage.

In re Marriage of Landfield, 153 Ill.Dec. 834, 567 N.E.2d 1061, 209 Ill.App.3d 678, appeal denied Landfield v. Landfield, 159 Ill.Dec. 109, 575 N.E.2d 916, 139 Ill.2d 597.

Ill.App. 1 Dist. 1990. Spouse seeking maintenance is not required to sell assets or impair capital in order to be maintained in manner established during marriage.

In re Marriage of Durante, 147 Ill.Dec. 56, 559 N.E.2d 56, 201 Ill.App.3d 376.

Ill.App. 1 Dist. 1990. Denial of maintenance to wife following dissolution of marriage that continued only slightly in excess of one year was not abuse of discretion, where wife was 37 years old at time of trial, enjoyed good health, and had not sacrificed any development of her career for benefit of husband. S.H.A. ch. 40, ¶ 504.

In re Marriage of Philips, 146 Ill.Dec. 191, 558 N.E.2d 154, 200 Ill.App.3d 395.

Ill.App. 1 Dist. 1989. Former wife was not entitled to maintenance absent showing that she lacked sufficient property, was unable to support herself, or was otherwise without sufficient income. S.H.A. ch. 40, ¶ 504(a).

In re Marriage of Koral, 141 Ill.Dec. 249, 551 N.E.2d 242, 194 Ill.App.3d 933.

Ill.App. 1 Dist. 1989. Trial court's denial of wife's request for maintenance was not abuse of discretion, inasmuch as assets awarded to wife generated income sufficient to meet her needs. S.H.A. ch. 40, ¶ 504(a).

In re Marriage of Harding, 136 Ill.Dec. 935, 545 N.E.2d 459, 189 Ill.App.3d 663.

Ill.App. 1 Dist. 1989. Maintenance was not unnecessary simply because sale of marital home could have generated substantial proceeds to support wife. S.H.A. ch. 40, ¶ 504.

In re Marriage of Dodge, 132 Ill.Dec. 700, 540 N.E.2d 440, 184 Ill.App.3d 495.

Wife has no obligation to sell her assets to generate income to support herself where husband has sufficient income to meet his needs while meeting hers. S.H.A. ch. 40, ¶ 504.

In re Marriage of Dodge, 132 Ill.Dec. 700, 540 N.E.2d 440, 184 Ill.App.3d 495.

Ill.App. 1 Dist. 1989. Wife's petition for maintenance was properly denied in light of evidence that she had income from business and tax-free income from trust in amount of $80,000

Figure 15

NATIVE VILLAGE OF EYAK, Appellant,

v.

GC CONTRACTORS, Appellee.

No. 6274.

Supreme Court of Alaska.

Jan. 14, 1983.

Suit was instituted by a native village to foreclose on a lien recorded by the contractor. The Superior Court, Third Judicial District, Milton M. Souter, J., entered judgment confirming an arbitration award in favor of contractor and rejected affirmative defense of immunity from suit, and native village appealed. The Supreme Court, Compton, J., held that: (1) the native village against which contractor sought to foreclose on a lien filed in connection with contract to build a community center for village was not immune from suit even if it was a federally recognized tribal entity since it agreed to submit to arbitration any disputes arising from the contract and thus waived whatever immunity it possessed; (2) the native village could waive tribal sovereign immunity without obtaining congressional authorization; (3) contract containing arbitration clause was not illegal because not approved by the Secretary of the Interior; and (4) arbitration clause was a sufficiently clear and unequivocal waiver of immunity to be effective.

Affirmed.

1. Indians ⚷27(1)

One of the sovereign privileges that Indian tribes possess is immunity from suit.

2. Indians ⚷27(1)

The native village against which contractor sought to foreclose on a lien filed in connection with contract to build a community center for village was not immune from suit even if it was a federally recognized tribal entity since it agreed to submit to arbitration any disputes arising from the contract and thus waived whatever immunity it possessed.

3. Appeal and Error ⚷854(1), 856(1)

The Supreme Court may affirm a judgment of the superior court on different grounds than those advanced by the superior court and even on grounds not raised by the parties in the superior court.

4. Indians ⚷27(1)

The phrase "without congressional authorization," within rule exempting all Indian nations from suit without congressional authorization, cannot be construed to mean that an Indian tribe is unable to waive its immunity.

5. Indians ⚷27(1)

An Indian tribe may waive its sovereign immunity without obtaining congressional authorization.

6. Indians ⚷24

Statute requiring the Secretary of the Interior to approve all contracts made by Indian tribes that relate to their tribal land or to claims against the United States was not applicable to contract between native village and contractor, even assuming native village was an Indian tribe, where contract involved construction of a community center on property leased from a third party and did not involve tribal land. 25 U.S.C.A. § 81.

7. Arbitration ⚷7.4

Any dispute arising from a contract cannot be resolved by arbitration, as specified in contract, if one of the parties intends to assert the defense of sovereign immunity.

8. Contracts ⚷143.5

To the extent possible, all provisions in a contract should be found meaningful.

9. Indians ⚷27(1)

A clause in a contract stating that the federal courts will resolve any disputes arising from the contract constitutes an express waiver of an Indian tribe's sovereign immunity and, with respect to an agreement that any dispute arising from a contract shall be resolved by the federal courts and an agree-

Figure 15 continued

ment that any dispute shall be resolved by arbitration, there is little substantive difference, and both appear to be clear indications that sovereign immunity has been waived.

10. Indians ⇐27(1)

Arbitration clause which was contained in contract calling for contractor to build a community center for a native village and which provided that disputes arising under the contract were to be resolved by arbitration amounted to an effective waiver of whatever immunity from suit the native village may have possessed.

Roger L. Hudson, Roberts & Shefelman, Anchorage, for appellant.

Kenneth O. Jarvi, Law Offices of Kenneth O. Jarvi, Anchorage, for appellee.

Robert E. Price, Asst. Atty. Gen., Wilson L. Condon, Atty. Gen., Juneau, for amicus curiae State of Alaska.

Before BURKE, C.J., RABINOWITZ and COMPTON, JJ., and DIMOND, Senior Justice.*

OPINION

COMPTON, Justice.

In this appeal, the Native Village of Eyak ("Eyak") contends that it is an "Indian tribe" and therefore immune from the suit brought against it by appellee GC Contractors. Eyak further contends that it did not waive its immunity by entering into a contract with GC Contractors containing an arbitration clause. We disagree with this contention. For the reasons set forth below, we conclude that it is not necessary to determine whether Eyak is an Indian tribe because, assuming that it is, Eyak waived whatever immunity it possessed when it agreed to resolve by arbitration any disputes that arose under its contract with GC Contractors.

I. FACTUAL AND PROCEDURAL BACKGROUND

In 1977, Eyak entered into a contract with GC Contractors, Inc., under which GC Contractors was to build a community center for Eyak on land leased by Eyak. The contract provided that disputes arising under it were to be resolved by arbitration. Eyak received a grant from the United States Economic Development Administration to pay for its community center.

Although GC Contractors completed construction of the community center, Eyak failed to pay $13,745.98 due under the contract. GC Contractors sued Eyak in the superior court to foreclose on a lien it had recorded. Eyak answered the complaint, denying it owed the money. It also asserted as affirmative defenses that it was immune from suit and that the parties had agreed by contract to submit disputes to arbitration. GC Contractors noticed the matter for arbitration and proceedings were subsequently held. Eyak again contended that it was immune from suit and argued that it would not be bound by the arbitration decision. The arbitrator impliedly rejected this argument and awarded GC Contractors the full sum sought.

GC Contractors requested confirmation of the award in the superior court. The court ruled that Eyak failed to establish that it is an Indian tribe and the court accordingly confirmed the arbitration award. Eyak appeals from this determination.

II. DISCUSSION

[1] Eyak's principal argument on appeal is that the superior court erred in ruling that it is not an Indian tribe. Indian tribes have been held to possess many but not all of the privileges of sovereignty that foreign nations and the United States hold. *E.g.*, *White Mountain Apache Tribe v. Bracker*, 448 U.S. 136, 142, 100 S.Ct. 2578, 2583, 65 L.Ed.2d 665, 671 (1980); *Santa Clara Pueblo v. Martinez*, 436 U.S. 49, 58, 98 S.Ct. 1670, 1677, 56 L.Ed.2d 106, 115 (1978); *United States v. Wheeler*, 435 U.S. 313, 322–26, 98

* Dimond, Senior Justice, sitting by assignment made pursuant to article IV, section 16, of the Constitution of Alaska and Alaska R.Admin.P. 23(a).

Table 1

Reporters

A. and A.2d	Atlantic Reporter	Connecticut, Delaware, District of Columbia, Maine, Maryland, New Hampshire, New Jersey, Pennsylvania, Rhode Island, Vermont
Cal. Rptr., Cal. Rptr.2d, and Cal. Rptr.3d	California Reporter	California
N.E. and N.E.2d	North Eastern Reporter	Illinois, Indiana, Massachusetts, New York, Ohio; also New York Court of Appeals
N.Y.S.	New York Supplement	New York
N.W. and N.W.2d	North Western Reporter	Iowa, Michigan, Minnesota, Nebraska, North Dakota, South Dakota, Wisconsin
P., P.2d, and P.3d	Pacific Reporter	Alaska, Arizona, California Supreme Court since 1960, Colorado, Hawaii, Idaho, Kansas, Montana, Nevada, New Mexico, Oklahoma, Oregon, Utah, Washington, Wyoming
S.E. and S.E.2d	South Eastern Reporter	Georgia, North Carolina, South Carolina, Virginia, West Virginia
So. and So.2d	Southern Reporter	Alabama, Florida, Louisiana, Mississippi
S.W., S.W.2d, and S.W.3d	South Western Reporter	Arkansas, Kentucky, Missouri, Tennessee, Texas

Table 2

Circuit Number/Name	Jurisdiction Covered/Location
1st	Maine, New Hampshire, Rhode Island, Massachusetts, Puerto Rico Location: Boston, MA
2nd	New York, Vermont, Connecticut Location: New York, NY
3rd	Pennsylvania, New Jersey, Delaware, Virgin Islands Location: Philadelphia, PA
4th	West Virginia, Virginia, Maryland, North Carolina, South Carolina Location: Richmond, VA
5th	Louisiana, Texas, Mississippi, Canal Zone (until given back to Panama) Location: New Orleans, LA
6th	Michigan, Ohio, Kentucky, Tennessee Location: Cincinnati, OH
7th	Wisconsin, Illinois, Indiana Location: Chicago, IL
8th	Minnesota, Iowa, Missouri, Arkansas, Nebraska, South Dakota, North Dakota Location: St. Louis, MO
9th	Hawaii, Washington, Oregon, Idaho, Montana, Nevada, Arizona, California, Alaska, Guam, N. Mariana Islands Location: San Francisco, CA
10th	Wyoming, Colorado, Utah, New Mexico, Kansas, Oklahoma Location: Denver, CO
11th	Alabama, Florida, Georgia (before October 1, 1981, this was part of the 5th circuit) Location: Atlanta, GA
District of Columbia	Washington, D.C.
Federal Circuit	Patent and Customs cases Location: Washington, D.C.

Shepard's Citations

As previously discussed, American jurisprudence is largely based on case law. Lawyers and judges look to *precedent* to determine what the law is—or is not—when a problem is presented to them. Precedent is a prior court decision that sets the example of the rule of law for the current decision. Like lawyers and judges, you have now done some case research and hopefully have found many cases that support your situation. How can you be sure that these cases are *good* law? How do you know that these cases have not been overruled or reversed? The answer is a *citator*—an index tool that provides citations of every case (or other authority) that cites your case. There are two principal citators—*Shepard's Citations* (both in print an online via LexisNexis) and *KeyCite* (an online-only service provided via Westlaw).

SHEPARD'S CITATIONS DEFINED

Shepard's, published by Shepard's/McGraw-Hill, is really nothing more than an index. When you look up a promising case in Shepard's, you are led to every single case that ever mentioned that case.

You have probably already read a few case opinions and noticed that judges cite other cases to support their arguments. Shepard's makes note of each case that is cited for any reason. Shepard's tells you if a case is overruled, reversed, explained, affirmed, or distinguished by these other cases. (see Figures 16 and 17 on pages 100–101.) Remember, a case will only be of value to you if it is still valid. Neglecting to use Shepard's could leave you with a position that is no longer of any legal significance. When you use Shepard's, you are never in doubt as to whether a case is still good law. This makes Shepard's an invaluable and necessary tool in legal research. You must master the art of *shepardizing* if you want to do effective case research.

WHICH SHEPARD'S TO USE

When you first glance inside the cover of a *Shepard's Citations*, you are likely to wince. It looks like hieroglyphics to the untrained eye. Do not let your initial reaction scare you. Once you understand what each column of numbers and letters is and how it works, using Shepard's is very easy.

A separate Shepard's is printed for each reporter. If you are shepardizing 742 N.E.2d 315, an Illinois case, you would choose the Shepard's for the North Eastern Reporter or for North Eastern Reporter, Illinois Cases (if available in your library). Collect all of the volumes for that Shepard's. Each library places their Shepard's in different places. Some place the Shepard's directly after the reporter series it supports. Others have all the Shepard's in one place.

Shepard's usually consists of maroon-colored hardbound volumes and at least one yellow-colored paper pamphlet. In addition, there may be a red-colored paper pamphlet, a plain paper pamphlet (the cover is paper-colored), and a blue-covered *Shepard's Express*. Take all the Shepard's volumes for that reporter and place them in chronological order.

How do you know you have all the proper volumes? Shepard's makes it easy. The newest paper pamphlet, whether yellow, red, or plain, always has a box on the front cover that says "What Your Library Should Contain." This will tell you exactly what that Shepard's set includes. (see Figure 18 on page 102.) Any other volumes or pamphlets will be extraneous and should not be used. This may be especially true of libraries that neglect to discard outdated paper pamphlets. Just follow the directions on the cover and you will not be misled.

HOW TO SHEPARDIZE A CASE

Once you have the Shepard's volumes in chronological order, you are ready to shepardize your case. Remember, for this example, you are shepardizing 742 N.E.2d 315 (called the *cited case*).

Realize that not all of Shepard's volumes will be helpful. Several volumes include citations for North Eastern Reporter, First Series only. You will want to set aside those volumes or any others that do not include your reporter volume. For example, if you are shepardizing a fairly new case, you may find that only the pamphlets include that case's reporter volume. You would set aside all of the hardbound volumes in that instance. When you shepardize, you always begin with the newest Shepard's volume, usually a paper pamphlet, and work backwards. This ensures that you are always finding the newest opinions that discuss the case you are interested in.

Now look at Figure 19 on page 103, illustrating a page from Shepard's North Eastern Reporter Citations. Notice that the volume number, 742, is in bold print. In Shepard's, the page number from the reporter is distinguished by dashes on either side of the number, in this case, "-315-." This is how you find the exact volume and page of the case you are shepardizing. All of the case citations following are other case opinions in which your case was cited. Newer volumes of Shepard's print the case name for easier identification.

First, you will want to look in the space before the citations. Do you see an *r*, *d*, *f*, or any other abbreviation that indicates case history or treatment? For example, 742 N.E.2d 315 has cases with an "f," meaning *followed*. This means that at 741 N.E.2d 988 (the citing case), the court followed the opinion as set out in the case, 742 N.E.2d 315 (again, called the cited case).

When you turn to page 988 of volume 742 of *North Eastern Reporter, Second Series*, you will immediately notice that you are in the middle of a case. Do not panic. You did not make a mistake. Shepard's brings you to the exact page where your case was cited. This is especially handy when the citing case is many pages long. You may not want to read the entire case to determine if it is really helpful. This allows you to look at the exact context in which your case was discussed. Once you determine that the case may be helpful, you will want to read the entire case to make sure it is going to aid your situation.

Now that you have checked one case, you may want to look at the other cases to determine if they also are helpful. Yet how do you decide which cases are better, particularly when you are relying on a popularly cited case? Shepard's may have hundreds of citations listed.

Look at Figure 20. Notice the superscribed numbers printed between the reporter abbreviation and the page number. This number refers to the *headnote*. Our illustration shows that 768 N.E.2d 98 specifically refers to headnote 8. The "8" refers to headnote 8 in 742 N.E.2d 315, your original case. If this headnote was especially helpful to your situation, you would look for any case in Shepard's making specific reference to that headnote. As you can see from Figure 20, other headnotes that were isolated were numbers 3, 6, and 7.

NOTE: *The blue-covered pamphlets called* ***Shepard's Express*** *are relatively new to the Shepard's family, and many older practitioners may not be very familiar with them. In an effort to get this information to you earlier (as much as three months), Shepard's notes whenever a case is cited but has not yet determined whether the citing case is overruling, distinguishing, reversing, affirming, and so on.*

If you find your case is cited in one of these cases, you will have to read the entire case and determine whether your case has been affected by the citing case.

HOW TO SHEPARDIZE A STATUTE

Shepardizing a statute follows the same basic rules as shepardizing a case. You obtain all the Shepard's volumes for your jurisdiction and separate the hardbound volumes pertaining to statutes and codes.

You will also need the pamphlets (yellow and red) as well. Statute information is toward the back of the pamphlet.

It is understandable why you would shepardize a case. Finding other cases in Shepard's gives you a chain of cases that are all interrelated. It is not immediately clear why you would shepardize a statute or code, but it is important to do so.

When you look up a statute or code in Shepard's, what you see first is legislative information about the statute. Has the statute been amended (A), added (Ad), or repealed (R)? Shepard's tells you (with the notations A, Ad, or R), along with the date of the change and where to locate the information in the session laws. (see Figures 21 and 22 on pages 105 and 106.) This will tell you at a glance whether or not the statute you are depending on is reliable.

After the legislative information, Shepard's cites to all cases that have construed or mentioned the statute. It will also tell you if a case has overruled the statute. In addition, Shepard's breaks down the statute into subdivisions. What this means is that if the portion of a statute applicable to your problem is 34.26(1)(a), you can shepardize for cases that construe not only 34.26, but 34.26(1) and 34.26(1)(a) specifically. This is important—not only will you have a valid statute, you will also have cases that are directly applicable to your situation. This information is at your fingertips without having to peruse pages and pages of statute annotations.

OTHER SHEPARD'S APPLICATIONS

Shepard's may be used for other sources as well. When you are shepardizing cases or statutes, you may find law review or *American Law Reports* (A.L.R.) citations. (see Chapter 6.) Additionally, both law reviews and A.L.R.'s have Shepard's of their own. The methodology is identical to shepardizing a case.

Figure 16

CASE ANALYSIS–ABBREVIATIONS

History of Cases

a	(affirmed)	On appeal, reconsideration or rehearing, the citing case affirms or adheres to the case you are *Shepardizing.*
cc	(connected case)	The citing case is related to the case you are *Shepardizing*, arising out of the same subject matter or involving the same parties.
D	(dismissed)	The citing case dismisses an appeal from the case you are *Shepardizing.*
De/ Cert den	(denied)	The citing case has denied further appeal in the case you are *Shepardizing.*
Gr	(granted)	The citing case has granted further appeal in the case you are *Shepardizing.*
m	(modified)	On appeal, reconsideration or rehearing, the citing case modifies or changes in some way, including affirmance in part and reversal in part, the case you are *Shepardizing.*
r	(reversed)	On appeal, reconsideration or rehearing, the citing case reverses the case you are *Shepardizing.*
ReD	(reh./recon. denied)	The citing order denies rehearing or reconsideration in the case you are *Shepardizing.*
ReG	(reh./recon. grated)	The citing order grants rehearing or reconsideration in the case you are *Shepardizing.*
s	(same case)	The citing case involves the same litigation as the case you are *Shepardizing*, but at a different stage of the proceedings.
S	(superseded)	On appeal, reconsideration or rehearing, the citing case supersedes or is substituted for the case you are *Shepardizing.*
TD	(transfer denied)	Transfer Denied by the Indiana Supreme Court.
TG	(transfer granted)	Transfer Granted by the Indiana Supreme Court.
US cert den		The citing order by the U. S. Supreme Court denies certiorari in the cases you are *Shepardizing.*
US cert dis		The citing order by the U. S. Supreme Court dismisses certiorari in the case you are *Shepardizing.*
US cert gran		The citing order by the U. S. Supreme Court grants certiorari in the case you are *Shepardizing.*
US reh den		The citing order by the U. S. Supreme Court denies rehearing in the case you are *Shepardizing.*
US reh dis		The citing order by the U. S. Supreme Court dismisses rehearing in the case you are *Shepardizing.*
v	(vacated)	The citing case vacates or withdraws the case you are *Shepardizing.*
W	(withdrawn)	The citing decision or opinion withdraws the decision or order you are *Shepardizing.*

Figure 17

CASE ANALYSIS–ABBREVIATIONS

Treatment of Cases

c	(criticized)	The citing opinion disagrees with the reasoning/result of the case you are *Shepardizing*, although the citing court may not have the authority to materially affect its precedential value.
ca	(conflicting authorities)	Among conflicting authorities as noted in cited case.
d	(distinguished)	The citing case differs from the case you are *Shepardizing*, either involving dissimilar facts or requiring a different application of the law.
e	(explained)	The citing opinion interprets or clarifies the case you are *Shepardizing* in a significant way.
f	(followed)	The citing opinion relies on the case you are *Shepardizing* as controlling or persuasive authority.
h	(harmonized)	The citing case differs from the case you are *Shepardizing*, but the citing court reconciles the difference or inconsistency in reaching its decision.
j	(dissenting opinion)	A dissenting opinion cites the case you are *Shepardizing*.
~	(concurring opinion)	A concurring opinion cites the case you are *Shepardizing*.
L	(limited)	The citing opinion restricts the application of the case you are *Shepardizing*, finding its reasoning applies only in specific limited circumstances.
o	(overruled)	The citing case expressly overrules or disapproves the case you are *Shepardizing*.
op	(overruled in part)	Ruling in the cited case overruled partially or on other grounds or with other qualifications.
q	(questioned)	The citing opinion questions the continuing validity or precedential value of the case you are *Shepardizing* because of intervening circumstances, including judicial or legislative overruling.
su	(superseded)	Superseded by statute as stated in cited case.

Other

#		The citing case is of questionable precedential value because review or rehearing has been granted by the California Supreme Court and/or the citing case has been ordered depublished pursuant to Rule 976 of the California Rules of Court. (Publication status should be verified before use of the citing case in California.)

For additional abbreviations on Case and Statutes Analysis, please refer to the Guide to *Shepard's*.

Figure 18

SHEPARD'S NORTHEASTERN REPORTER CITATIONS

Cumulative Supplement

WHAT YOUR LIBRARY SHOULD CONTAIN

1995 Bound Volume (Volumes 1-11)
1995–1999 Bound Supplement (Volumes 1 and 2)
1999–2002 Bound Supplement (Volumes 1 and 2)
2002–2004 Bound Supplement (Volumes 1 and 2)

**Supplemented with:*
–May 2005 Annual Cumulative Supplement Vol. 97 No. 5
–September 2005 Cumulative Supplement Vol. 97 No. 9

DISCARD ALL OTHER ISSUES

Figure 19

Vol. 742 **NORTHEASTERN REPORTER, 2d SERIES**

f = followed

headnote reference

j = dissenting opinion

De 738NE383

—183—
Rizvi v State Med. Bd.
2000
(138OA3d682)
De 738NE384
s 736NE26
cc 765NE395

—188—
Carosella v Conwell
2000
(138OA3d688)
De 738NE1256

—192—
Hohmann, Boukis & Curtis Co. v Brunn
2000
(138OA3d693)

—196—
City of Middleburg Heights v D'Ettorre
2000
(138OA3d700)
De 738NE380

—203—
Selker & Furber v Brightman
2000
(138OA3d710)

—206—
State v Walters
2000
(138OA3d715)

—209—
Baycliffs Corp. v Village of Marblehead
2000
(138OA3d719)

—219—
Larkins v State Dep't of Rehab. & Corr.
2000
(138OA3d733)

—222—
Brewster v CSX Transp., Inc.
2000
(138OA3d738)

—224—
City of Brook Park v Kirsch
2000
(138OA3d741)

—228—
American Watchmakers-Clockmakers Inst., Inc. v Tracy
2000
(138OA3d747)

—232—
City of Dublin v State
2000
(138OA3d753)

—238—
Hayes v State Med. Bd.
2000
(138OA3d762)
De 741NE143
cc 689NE547

—247—
In re McCoy
2000
(138OA3d774)

—251—
People v Mahaffey
2000
(194Il2d154)
(252IlD1)
US cert den
151LE439
US cert den
122SC565
cc 539NE1172
cc 651NE1055
cc 516US1002
cc 133LE450
cc 116SC547
745NE1200
745NE1250
f 749NE[11]943
f 749NE944
752NE[22]498
755NE88
756NE[20]46

—269—
People v McNeal
2000
(194Il2d135)
(252IlD19)
cc 677NE841
cc 703NE35
cc 522US917
cc 139LE235
cc 118SC304

—279—
Garibaldi v Applebaum
2000
(194Il2d438)
(252IlD29)
s 653NE42
s 704NE698
cc 660NE1268
763NE[3]899

—287—
People v Scott
2000
(194Il2d268)
(252IlD37)
US cert den
151LE115
US cert den
122SC168
cc 594NE217
cc 507US989
cc 123LE156
cc 113SC1590
~ 757NE[19]457
95AL5137n

—299—
People v Ruiz
2000
(194Il2d454)
(252IlD49)
cc 447NE148
cc 479NE922
cc 547NE170
cc 686NE574
cc 688NE658
cc 77LE1341
cc 110LE652
cc 103SC2465
cc 110SC2632
Cir. 7
149FS2d538

—306—
People v Sutherland
2000
(194Il2d289)
(252IlD56)

—315—
People v Strain
2000
(194Il2d467)
(252IlD65)
s 714NE74
f 741NE988
744NE897
f 744NE1270
~ 749NE367
753NE1099
~ 760NE511
j 762NE1110
Cir. 7
246F3d940

—326—
Berry v Juergensmeyer
2000
(192Il2d685)
(252IlD76)

—326—
Choice Props. v Krulas
2000
(192Il2d686)
(252IlD76)

—326—
Cosgrove v Commonwealth Edison Co.
2000
(192Il2d686)
(252IlD76)
s 734NE155

—326—
Chicago Fire Fighters Union Local No. 2 v City of Chicago
2000
(192Il2d686)
(252IlD76)
s 735NE108
s 751NE1169

—326—
City of Chicago v Moore
2000
(192Il2d686)
(252IlD76)

—326—
Chaney v Yetter Mfg. Co.
2000
(192Il2d685)
(252IlD76)
s 734NE1028

—326—
Corluka v Bridgford Foods
2000
(192Il2d686)
(252IlD76)

—326—
Carter v Wittenborn
2000
(192Il2d685)
(252IlD76)

—326—
City of Chicago v Marquette Nat'l Bank
2000
(192Il2d686)
(252IlD76)

—326—
Chanthaboury v Universal Fire & Cas. Ins. Co.
2000
(192Il2d686)
(252IlD76)

—326—
Allen v Illinois Community College Bd.
2000
(192Il2d685)
(252IlD76)
s 734NE926

—326—
Country Mut. Ins. Co. v Federated Mut. Ins. Co.
2000
(192Il2d686)
(252IlD76)
s 735NE1045

—326—
Broadway Produce, Inc. v Fidelity & Cas. Co.
2000
(192Il2d685)
(252IlD76)

—326—
Belleville Toyota, Inc. v Toyota Motor Sales
2000
(192Il2d685)
(252IlD76)
s 738NE938

—326—
Bishop v We Care Hair Dev. Corp.
2000
(192Il2d685)
(252IlD76)
s 738NE610
Cir. 9
24Fed Appx
[795

—326—
Country Mut. Ins. Co. v Universal Underwriters Ins. Co.
2000
(192Il2d686)
(252IlD76)
s 735NE1032

—326—
Baggett v Industrial Comm'n (Marion Community Sch. Dist. No. 2)
2000
(192Il2d685)
(252IlD76)

—326—
American Legion Post No. 32 v Zehnder
2000
(192Il2d685)
(252IlD76)

—326—
Citizens' Util. Bd. v Illinois Commerce Comm'n
2000
(192Il2d686)
(252IlD76)
s 735NE92

—327—
Holtzman v Holtzman
2000
(192Il2d688)
(252IlD77)

—327—
Crystal Lake Enters. v Grand Nat'l Bank
2000
(192Il2d687)
(252IlD77)

—327—
Horbach v Gardner, Carton & Douglas
2000
(192Il2d688)
(252IlD77)

—327—
Griffith v Pembroke Twp.
2000
(192Il2d687)
(252IlD77)
s 732NE16

—327—
People v B.L. (In re B.L.)
2000
(192Il2d688)

Figure 20

Vol. 742 **NORTHEASTERN REPORTER, 2d SERIES**

—89—
785NE1256
Md
808A2d827
—96—
Commonwealth v Sanchez
De 810NE1230
—98—
2004NY LX[3] [1608
2004NYMisc [LX957
2004NYMisc [LX1138
786NE[5]19
803NE[5]366
803NE[3]377
803NE[4]377
j 809NE627
809NE[5]654
744NYS2d602
745NYS2d115
745NYS2d198
749NYS2d308
749NYS2d590
750NYS2d38
750NYS2d[1] [163
750NYS2d[3] [354
750NYS2d[5] [354
753NYS2d608
754NYS2d[4] [822
755NYS2d790
756NYS2d[5] [120
757NYS2d203
759NYS2d791
763NYS2d[3] [356
765NYS2d[3] [133
768NYS2d357
771NYS2d[5]45
771NYS2d[3]56
771NYS2d[4]56
d 773NYS2d [266
773NYS2d779
773NYS2d[2] [780
773NYS2d[2] [897
777NYS2d159
j 777NYS2d398
777NYS2d[5] [425
777NYS2d842
778NYS2d396
Cir. 2
272FS2d344
—106—
745NYS2d198
768NYS2d358
778NYS2d396
—107—
741NYS2d226
—109—
Cir. 2
2003USDist [LX6254
—114—
s 2000NY LX [1417
s 2000NY LX [3495
2004NYMisc [LX672
2004NYMisc [LX1216
803NE[8]373
737NYS2d739
757NYS2d[3] [364
757NYS2d670
f 761NYS2d[2] [506
763NYS2d395
771NYS2d[8]52
771NYS2d[4] [563
—119—
Bottom v Goord
s 2001NY LX [169
—121—
Katsorhis v City of New York Conflicts of Interest Bd.
s 2000NY App [Div LX7983
—121—
Kuttemperoor v Mount Sinai Med. Ctr.
s 2000NY App [Div LX7999
—123—
Montecalvo v Columbia County
758NYS2d297
—123—
Baltia Air Lines, Inc. v CIBC Oppenheimer Corp.
s 2000NY App [Div LX8778
—123—
Acunto v New York State Div. of Hous. & Community Renewal
s 2000NY App [Div LX7286
—124—
784NE[1]205
d 784NE207
—127—
786NE511
—130—
State ex rel. Swingle v Zaleski
cc 2002USDist [LX16064
cc 215FS2d919
768NE[2]1177
797NE983
—144—
State v Mitts
cc 784NE698
—144—
State v Swingle
cc 2002USDist [LX16064
cc 215FS2d919
—145—
State v Yarbrough
s 772NE641
s 805NE535
—145—
Parrish v Parrish
s 767NE1182
—146—
Hamilton Ins. Serv. v Nationwide Ins. Cos.
cc 2002Ohio LX [1684
—147—
Medina County Bar Ass'n v Muhlbach
s 2001Ohio LX [894
—148—
Cuyahoga County Bar Ass'n v Nigolian
s 776NE493
—148—
Cuyahoga County Bar Ass'n v Muhlbach
s 2001Ohio LX [895
—164—
f 2004OhioMisc [LX374
778NE[3]1080
778NE1099
798NE659
f 798NE660
809NE[1]53
Cir. 6
2001USDist [LX22655
2003USDist [LX15347
252FS2d537
102ALR5 11n
—192—
d 790NE348
—224—
795NE[2]1250
—238—
S D
d 645NW606
—251—
US cert den
534US1029
Reh den
2001Ill LX217
cc 294F3d907
cc 2001USDist [LX18934
772NE[3]766
772NE[10]767
773NE[3]19
778NE[4]225
778NE[15]1190
781NE[3]607
781NE[4]607
783NE[3]138
783NE[22]653
785NE[1]883
787NE[6]266
f 792NE278
793NE18
793NE[8]202
793NE[4]620
793NE660
794NE[4]163
794NE[4]304
794NE[1]323
f 794NE[4]323
794NE[4]335
794NE[2]373
795NE[4]865
801NE104
801NE[2]1047
801NE[1]1048
803NE111
807NE645
Cir. 7
245FS2d934
—269—
Reh den
2001Ill LX235
2004Ill LX[1]371
2004Ill LX[4]371
f 2004Ill LX371
2004IllApp LX [955
789NE[6]930
~ 791NE503
~f 791NE504
792NE[11]535
793NE[5]8
799NE[2]956
802NE[6]1244
807NE503
807NE650
808NE1116
809NE1236
f 809NE1239
—279—
Reh den
2001Ill LX227
2004Ill LX676
j 2004Ill LX676
N C
f 573SE598
—287—
US cert den
534US873
Reh den
2001Ill LX219
f 785NE891
785NE[34]891
801NE560
802NE265
808NE1116
—299—
Reh den
2001Ill LX228
cc 794NE251
j 2001Ill LX5
j 770NE212
—306—
Reh den
2001Ill LX220
—315—
Reh den
2001Ill LX230
2004IllApp LX [788
2004IllApp LX [818
d 768NE98
768NE[8]98
771NE28
771NE[7]30
e 771NE34
771NE[8]34
772NE[6]832
d 774NE422
774NE[7]422
793NE22
801NE102
801NE[8]107
810NE[3]183
f 810NE186
d 810NE187
e 810NE188
Colo
60P3d734
Conn
d 835A2d459
—328—
James v Covenant Med. Ctr.
s 776NE350
—329—
McGreevy v Roland Mach. Co.
s 776NE350
—330—
People v Caffey
cc 2003USDist [LX2085
—330—
People v Bustami
s 757NE127
—331—
People v Etherly
s 801NE99
—331—
People v Gostele
s 2000IllApp [LX498
—331—
People v Fitts
s 764NE611
—331—
People v Gordon
s 777NE1085
—332—
People v Mamo
cc 2001USDist [LX14056
—333—
People v Rollins
s 757NE128
—333—
People v Sherman
US cert den
534US907
US reh den
535US1013

332

page #
case name of cited case
d = distinguished
e = explained
headnote references

Figure 21

ABBREVIATIONS—ANALYSIS STATUTES

Form of Statute

Amend.	Amendment	¶	Paragraph
Art.	Article	P.L.	Public Law
C or Ch.	Chapter	Proc.	Proclamation
CCJR	Conference Committee Joint Resolution	Res.	Resolution
		§	Section
Cl.	Clause	S. B.	Senate Bill
Ex.	Extra Session	S. C. R.	Senate Concurrent Resolution
Ex. Ord.	Executive Order		
H. B.	House Bill	S. J. R.	Senate Joint Resolution
H. C. R.	House Concurrent Resolution	S. M.	Senate Memorial
		Sp	Special Acts or Laws
H. J. R.	House Joint Resolution	S. R.	Senate Resolution
H. M.	House Memorial	St.	Statutes at Large
H. R.	House Resolution	Stat.	Florida Statutes
J. R.	Joint Resolution	Subd.	Subdivision
No.	Number	Sub ¶	Subparagraph
p	Page	Subsec.	Subsection

Operation of Statute

Legislative

A	(amended)	Statute amended.
Ad	(added)	New section added.
E	(extended)	Provisions of an existing statute extended in their application to a later statute, or allowance of additional time for performance of duties required by a statute within a limited time.
L	(limited)	Provisions of an existing statute declared not to be extended in their application to a later statute.
R	(repealed)	Abrogation of an existing statute.
Re-en	(re-enacted)	Statute re-enacted.
Rn	(renumbered)	Renumbering of existing sections.
Rp	(repealed in part)	Abrogation of part of an existing statute.
Rs	(repealed and superseded)	Abrogation of an existing statute and substitution of new legislation therefor.
Rv	(revised)	Statute revised.
S	(superseded)	Substitution of new legislation for an existing statute not expressly abrogated.
Sd	(suspended)	Statute suspended.
Sdp	(suspended in part)	Statute suspended in part.
Sg	(supplementing)	New matter added to an existing statute.
Sp	(superseded in part)	Substitution of new legislation for part of an existing statute expressly abrogated.
Va	(validated)	

Judicial

C	Constitutional.	V	Void or invalid.
U	Unconstitutional.	Va	Valid.
Up	Unconstitutional in part.	Vp	Void or invalid in part.

ABBREVIATIONS—COURTS

Cir. DC–U.S. Court of Appeals, District of Columbia Circuit
Cir. (number)–U.S. Court of Appeals Circuit (number)
Cir. Fed.–U.S. Court of Appeals, Federal Circuit
CCPA–Court of Customs and Patents Appeals
CIT–United States Court of International Trade
ClCt–Claims Court (U.S.)
CtCl–Court of Claims (U.S.)
CuCt–Customs Court
ECA–Temporary Emergency Court of Appeals
ML–Judicial Panel on Multidistrict Litigation
RRR–Special Court Regional Rail Reorganization Act of 1973

Figure 22

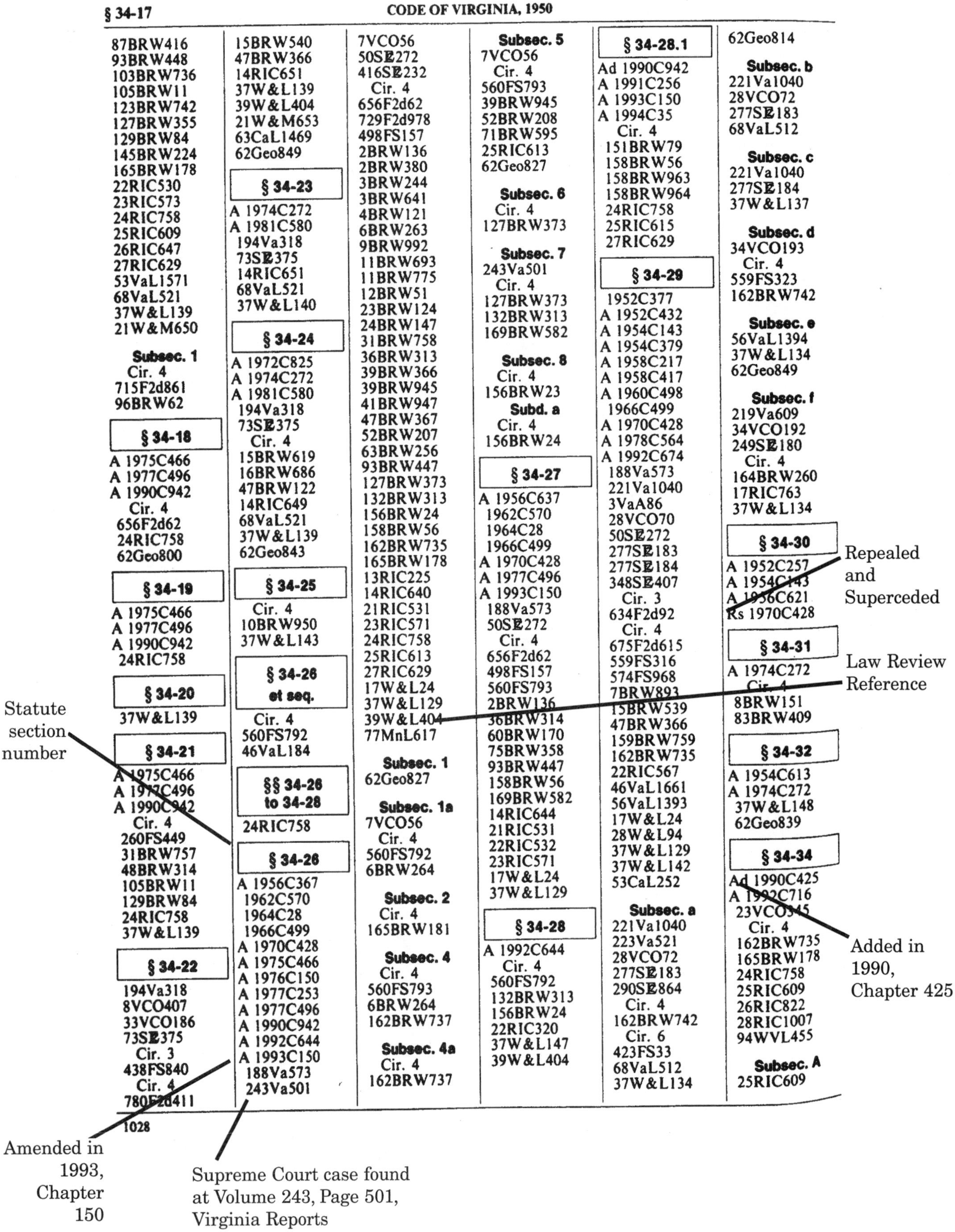

§ 34-17 CODE OF VIRGINIA, 1950

87BRW416
93BRW448
103BRW736
105BRW11
123BRW742
127BRW355
129BRW84
145BRW224
165BRW178
22RIC530
23RIC573
24RIC758
25RIC609
26RIC647
27RIC629
53VaL1571
68VaL521
37W&L139
21W&M650

Subsec. 1
Cir. 4
715F2d861
96BRW62

§ 34-18
A 1975C466
A 1977C496
A 1990C942
Cir. 4
656F2d62
24RIC758
62Geo800

§ 34-19
A 1975C466
A 1977C496
A 1990C942
24RIC758

§ 34-20
37W&L139

§ 34-21
A 1975C466
A 1977C496
A 1990C942
Cir. 4
260FS449
31BRW757
48BRW314
105BRW11
129BRW84
24RIC758
37W&L139

§ 34-22
194Va318
8VCO407
33VCO186
73SE375
Cir. 3
438FS840
Cir. 4
780F2d411

15BRW540
47BRW366
14RIC651
37W&L139
39W&L404
21W&M653
63CaL1469
62Geo849

§ 34-23
A 1974C272
A 1981C580
194Va318
73SE375
14RIC651
68VaL521
37W&L140

§ 34-24
A 1972C825
A 1974C272
A 1981C580
194Va318
73SE375
Cir. 4
15BRW619
16BRW686
47BRW122
14RIC649
68VaL521
37W&L139
62Geo843

§ 34-25
Cir. 4
10BRW950
37W&L143

§ 34-26 et seq.
Cir. 4
560FS792
46VaL184

§§ 34-26 to 34-28
24RIC758

§ 34-26
A 1956C367
1962C570
1964C28
1966C499
A 1970C428
A 1975C466
A 1976C150
A 1977C253
A 1977C496
A 1990C942
A 1992C644
A 1993C150
188Va573
243Va501

7VCO56
50SE272
416SE232
Cir. 4
656F2d62
729F2d978
498FS157
2BRW136
2BRW380
3BRW244
3BRW641
4BRW121
6BRW263
9BRW992
11BRW693
11BRW775
12BRW51
23BRW124
24BRW147
31BRW758
36BRW313
39BRW366
39BRW945
41BRW947
47BRW367
52BRW207
63BRW256
93BRW447
127BRW373
132BRW313
156BRW24
158BRW56
162BRW735
165BRW178
13RIC225
14RIC640
21RIC531
23RIC571
24RIC758
25RIC613
27RIC629
17W&L24
37W&L129
39W&L404
77MnL617

Subsec. 1
62Geo827

Subsec. 1a
7VCO56
Cir. 4
560FS792
6BRW264

Subsec. 2
Cir. 4
165BRW181

Subsec. 4
Cir. 4
560FS793
6BRW264
162BRW737

Subsec. 4a
Cir. 4
162BRW737

Subsec. 5
7VCO56
Cir. 4
560FS793
39BRW945
52BRW208
71BRW595
25RIC613
62Geo827

Subsec. 6
Cir. 4
127BRW373

Subsec. 7
243Va501
Cir. 4
127BRW373
132BRW313
169BRW582

Subsec. 8
Cir. 4
156BRW23

Subd. a
Cir. 4
156BRW24

§ 34-27
A 1956C637
1962C570
1964C28
1966C499
A 1970C428
A 1977C496
A 1993C150
188Va573
50SE272
Cir. 4
656F2d62
498FS157
560FS793
2BRW136
36BRW314
60BRW170
75BRW358
93BRW447
158BRW56
169BRW582
14RIC644
21RIC531
22RIC532
23RIC571
17W&L24
37W&L129

§ 34-28
A 1992C644
Cir. 4
560FS792
132BRW313
156BRW24
22RIC320
37W&L147
39W&L404

§ 34-28.1
Ad 1990C942
A 1991C256
A 1993C150
A 1994C35
Cir. 4
151BRW79
158BRW56
158BRW963
158BRW964
24RIC758
25RIC615
27RIC629

§ 34-29
1952C377
A 1952C432
A 1954C143
A 1954C379
A 1958C217
A 1958C417
A 1960C498
1966C499
A 1970C428
A 1978C564
A 1992C674
188Va573
221Va1040
3VaA86
28VCO70
50SE272
277SE183
277SE184
348SE407
Cir. 3
634F2d92
Cir. 4
675F2d615
559FS316
574FS968
7BRW893
15BRW539
47BRW366
159BRW759
162BRW735
22RIC567
46VaL1661
56VaL1393
17W&L24
28W&L94
37W&L129
37W&L142
53CaL252

Subsec. a
221Va1040
223Va521
28VCO72
277SE183
290SE864
Cir. 4
162BRW742
Cir. 6
423FS33
68VaL512
37W&L134

62Geo814

Subsec. b
221Va1040
28VCO72
277SE183
68VaL512

Subsec. c
221Va1040
277SE184
37W&L137

Subsec. d
34VCO193
Cir. 4
559FS323
162BRW742

Subsec. e
56VaL1394
37W&L134
62Geo849

Subsec. f
219Va609
34VCO192
249SE180
Cir. 4
164BRW260
17RIC763
37W&L134

§ 34-30
A 1952C257
A 1954C143
A 1956C621
Rs 1970C428

§ 34-31
A 1974C272
Cir. 4
8BRW151
83BRW409

§ 34-32
A 1954C613
A 1974C272
37W&L148
62Geo839

§ 34-34
Ad 1990C425
A 1992C716
23VCO345
Cir. 4
162BRW735
165BRW178
24RIC758
25RIC609
26RIC822
28RIC1007
94WVL455

Subsec. A
25RIC609

1028

Repealed and Superceded
Law Review Reference
Statute section number
Added in 1990, Chapter 425
Amended in 1993, Chapter 150
Supreme Court case found at Volume 243, Page 501, Virginia Reports

American Law Reports

American Law Reports, or A.L.R. as they are more commonly known, are sets of books published by Lawyers Cooperative Publishing Company that report on specific legal topics. These reports are known as *annotations,* but should not be confused with annotations in statutes and codes. Unlike those in statutes and codes, A.L.R. annotations are not just abstracts, or summaries, about cases.

Instead, A.L.R. annotations are comprehensive studies on the topics chosen. Each report is illustrated by a case opinion, which the editors believe would be of importance to lawyers and other legal professionals. Although the illustrative case opinions originally preceded each annotation, they are now (beginning with A.L.R.5th) found in a separate section in the back of each volume. Each annotation expounds on the issue printed by the court in each of the illustrative cases.

The annotations track the development of the issue from its beginnings in our legal system to the date of publication. This is done by citing and analyzing other cases from all jurisdictions that discuss or relate to the issue in the printed case. These annotations are sweeping reports on important issues, and can be a wealth of information if they pertain to your problem. (see Figure 23 on pages 112–115.)

HOW TO FIND AMERICAN LAW REPORTS

American Law Reports are printed in eight sets: *American Law Reports* (abbreviated A.L.R.); *American Law Reports, Second Series* (abbreviated A.L.R.2d, and sometimes referred to as "Second Series"); *American Law Reports, Third Series* (A.L.R.3d or "Third Series"); *American Law Reports, Fourth Series* (A.L.R.4th or "Fourth Series"); *American Law Reports, Fifth Series* (A.L.R.5th or "Fifth Series"); *American Law Reports, Sixth Series* (A.L.R.6th or "Sixth Series"); *American Law Reports, Federal* (A.L.R. Fed.); and, *American Law Reports, Federal, Second Series* (A.L.R. Fed. 2d).

How would you find an annotation pertaining to your particular problem? You certainly would not want to start with volume one of A.L.R. (first series) and work your way through each set. A digest will not help you, and neither will the topic and key number system. There are multiple research methods that will lead you to an annotation.

The Index Method

A.L.R. comes complete with a multiple volume index that covers all the sets with the exception of A.L.R. (first series), which is indexed separately. These indices are updated by pocket parts printed annually. (see Figure 24 on page 116.)

Searching by the index method requires you to follow the information on how to search in an index in Chapter 1. As you can see in Figure 24, the index lists all annotations pertaining to the topic—in this case, alimony. If you were interested in the annotation circled, you would go to Volume 98 of A.L.R.3d at page 453.

NOTE: *Page 453 refers to the first page of the annotation, not the case. You must go back to page 445 to read the case that is the basis for the annotation.*

The Digest Method

A.L.R. also comes with a set of digests. A.L.R. First Series and Second Series have their own digests, while the Third, Fourth, Fifth, and Sixth Series, A.L.R. Federal, and A.L.R. Federal 2d are combined. (see Figure 25 on page 117.) As you can see, the digests are separated into topics. In this case, when you look up *alimony*, you are referred to *divorce and separation*. Each topic begins with an index to the annotations, and lists abstracts of cases printed in the volumes as well as any annotations that pertain directly to that topic.

Shepard's Citator Method

Shepard's lists any A.L.R. annotation that cites the case you are shepardizing. For example, the cases outlined in Figure 26 (on page 118), make reference to multiple A.L.R. citations. Additionally, Shepard's has a citator dedicated solely to American Law Reports. You may want to use Shepard's if you believe you have exhausted your other avenues of case method searching. (See Chapter 5 for specific instructions on how to shepardize.) Be aware that Shepard's for American Law Reports is not printed in the usual color scheme for Shepard's. All volumes are in the same greenish-olive color of American Law Reports instead.

UPDATING AMERICAN LAW REPORTS

American Law Reports has gone through many mutations regarding its method of updating. Do not let this confuse you. It may help to think of each series as a separate set of books.

Blue Book of Supplemental Decisions

These volumes supplement A.L.R. (first series). When you locate an annotation in A.L.R. (first series), you then go to the A.L.R. *Blue Book* and look up that citation again. It will cite all other cases that have been written since the original annotation. For example, look at Figure 27 on page 119. Once you obtain these citations, you can look them up and determine if the law has changed since the annotation in A.L.R. (first series) was written. The *Blue Book of Supplemental Decisions* is updated by an annual pamphlet.

A.L.R.2d Later Case Service

American Law Reports, Second Series, does not use the Blue Book of Supplemental Decisions. Instead, it is updated by the *Later Case Service*. Unlike the Blue Book of Supplemental Decisions, it not only lists any case citations that arose since the publication of an annotation, it also digests the cases and indexes them to the exact section of the A.L.R.2d annotation they are meant to update. This enables you to see directly where the law has been expanded or changed. (see Figure 28 on page 120.)

Pocket Parts

Cases that update the annotations in A.L.R.3d, A.L.R.4th, A.L.R.5th, A.L.R.6th, A.L.R. Fed., and A.L.R. Fed. 2d may be found in annual *pocket part supplements*. You will not need to consult a separate set of books like for A.L.R. First Series and Second Series. You use the pocket part in the same manner as you do for digests.

One important point to remember about A.L.R.6th and A.L.R. Fed. 2d is that new volumes are still being published. You will need to consult any new volumes printed after the date of the pocket part to determine if there is updated information on any topic that is not reflected in the pocket part.

Superseding Annotations

Assume that you found an annotation in A.L.R.2d. Later cases (found in the Later Case Service) indicate that the issue discussed in the annotation has been completely changed by the newer case opinions. The annotation in A.L.R.2d, while giving you a foundation for your problem and historical background of the law, will not be helpful.

It would be helpful to find out if the American Law Reports editors wrote a new annotation—one that discusses the law in the past (superceded) *and* currently (supplemented). There are two ways to see if the annotation was either *superseded* or *supplemented*.

One is to look up the annotation as you would to update for newer cases. The Blue Book of Supplemental Decisions, A.L.R.2d Later Case Service, and pocket parts for A.L.R.3d, A.L.R.4th, A.L.R.5th, and A.L.R. Fed. all refer to the latest annotations available on the same topic. In addition, you may refer to the *Annotation History Table*. This table is found in the last volume of the *Index to Annotations*. (see Figure 29 on page 121.) If the table says "supplemented," you will read both annotations, while if it says "superseded," you would only have to read the newer annotation. Most annotations in A.L.R.3d, A.L.R.4th, A.L.R.5th, and A.L.R. Fed. will be superseded instead of merely supplemented. Most supplemented materials refer to A.L.R. First Series and Second Series.

For example, as shown in Figure 29, 90 A.L.R.4th 586 was superseded by 72 A.L.R.5th 403. You only need to read 72 A.L.R.5th 403 to get the full import of the topic being discussed in the annotation. If, however, it had said "supplemented" you would have had to read both 90 A.L.R.4th 586 and 72 A.L.R.5th 403.

American Law Reports can be a very helpful resource for you. It is most helpful when you know what your problem is really about. Then

A.L.R. may give you an abundance of information, covering your issue in minute detail. It is also beneficial, however, when you only have a vague idea about what your problem entails. The annotations may help you frame your issue more clearly. After reading an annotation, you may get more ideas, learn more words and phrases concerning your problem, and want to go back to doing case research in the digests. Sometimes all your research will need to get on the right course is someone else's point of view on a subject. American Law Reports' annotations provides that point of view.

Figure 23

ANNOTATION

DIVORCED WOMAN'S SUBSEQUENT SEXUAL RELATIONS OR MISCONDUCT AS WARRANTING, ALONE OR WITH OTHER CIRCUMSTANCES, MODIFICATION OF ALIMONY DECREE

TOTAL CLIENT-SERVICE LIBRARY® REFERENCES

24 Am Jur 2d, Divorce and Separation §§ 685–88

8 Am Jur Pl & Pr Forms (rev), Divorce and Separation, Forms 611-16

1 Am Jur Legal Forms 2d, Alimony and Separation Agreements §§ 17:21–17:26, 17:71–17:83

1 Am Jur Proof of Facts 237, Adultery; 1 Am Jur Proof of Facts 421, Alimony, Proof 4; 17 Am Jur Proof of Facts 2d 345, Forensic Economics—Use of Economists in Cases of Dissolution of Marriage

17 Am Jur Trials 721, Defense Against Wife's Action for Support

US L Ed Digest, Divorce and Separation § 8

ALR Digests, Divorce and Separation §§ 95–105

L Ed Index to Annos, Divorce and Separation

ALR Quick Index, Alimony; Divorce and Separation; Sexual Relations and Offenses; Subsequent Acts or Events

Federal Quick Index, Alimony; Divorce and Separation; Sexual Relations and Offenses

Consult POCKET PART in this volume for later cases

453

Figure 23 continued

INDEX

Figure 23 continued

Since relevant statutes are included only to the extent that they are reflected in the reported cases within the scope of this annotation, the reader is advised to consult the latest enactments of pertinent jurisdictions.

[b] Related matters

Adulterous wife's right to permanent alimony. 86 ALR3d 97.

Fault as consideration in alimony, spousal support, or property division awards pursuant to no-fault divorce. 86 ALR3d 1116.

Divorce: Power of court to modify decree to alimony or support of spouse which was based on agreement of parties. 61 ALR3d 520.

Retrospective increase in allowance for alimony, separate maintenance, or support. 52 ALR3d 156.

Effect of remarriage of spouses to each other on permanent alimony provisions in final divorce decree. 52 ALR3d 1334.

Alimony as affected by wife's remarriage, in absence of controlling specific statute. 48 ALR2d 270.

Remarriage of wife as affecting husband's obligation under separation agreement to support her or make other money payments to her. 48 ALR2d 318.

Reconciliation as affecting decree for alimony. 35 ALR2d 741.

Change in financial condition or needs of husband or wife as ground for modification of decree for alimony or maintenance. 18 ALR2d 10.

Misconduct of wife to whom divorce is decreed as affecting allowance of alimony, or amount allowed. 9 ALR2d 1026.

Husband's default, contempt, or other misconduct as affecting modification of decree for alimony, separate maintenance, or support. 6 ALR2d 835.

Retrospective modification of or refusal to enforce decree for alimony, separate maintenance, or support. 6 ALR2d 1277.

Wife's misconduct or fault as affecting her right to temporary alimony or suit money. 2 ALR2d 307.

§ 2. Summary and comment

[a] Generally

Generally, where statutes allow modification, both judicially determined alimony awards and those based on contractual provisions incorporated in a decree are modifiable by the court where there has been a substantial change in the circumstances of at least one of the parties.[7] Usually the change in circumstances required is a financial one, but the divorced wife's subsequent sexual relations or misconduct may warrant, in itself, or in combination with other circumstances, the modification of an alimony decree, as shown by the cases discussed in this annotation.

The courts have frequently decided or discussed the question whether a finding of extramarital sexual relations on the part of a divorced wife warranted or was relevant to a modification of a decree for alimony, both under and in the absence of applicable statutory provisions.[8] Where the former wife was living with another, one of two general types of statutory provisions were involved. Under one type of statute allowing modification for cohabitation without any further requirements, the former wife's con-

ments are often brought as suits to modify private contract obligations, and are thus not within the scope of this annotation.

7. See generally, 24 Am Jur 2d, Divorce and Separation §§ 675 et seq.

8. §§ 3–11, infra.

Figure 23 continued

duct in living with a paramour has been held sufficient to warrant, or to be relevant to, modification of the decree.[9] Under the second type of statute, which allowed modification for cohabitation of an ex-wife with a lover and also required that she hold herself out as her lover's wife, it has been held that the former wife's conduct was sufficient to warrant, or was relevant to, modification;[10] and her conduct has also been held to be insufficient, under the circumstances involved, to authorize or affect such modification.[11] Specific circumstances resulting in such a holding include a separation agreement which was stipulated to be nonmodifiable,[12] but not when the former wife's lover was a lesbian, since then the relationship did not fall within the statutory requirement that the woman live with a man and hold herself out as his wife.[13]

Where no specific statutory provisions were applicable and where no changes in financial circumstances were shown, the former wife's conduct in living with a lover was held sufficient to warrant, or to be relevant to, modification of a decree for alimony,[14] although it has also frequently been held to be insufficient.[15]

Where changed financial circumstances were also present, courts have held that the former wife's conduct in living with a lover warranted, or was relevant to, modification of the decree, not only where the changed financial circumstances involved their relationship, as where the former wife was receiving support from her lover[16] or was supporting him,[17] but also where the change in financial circumstances did not involve their relationship.[18]

Where the former wife has indulged in sexual relations without cohabitation, this has been held both sufficient[19] and insufficient[20] to warrant, or to be relevant to, modification of a decree for alimony. But where the sexual relations have occurred in combination with changed financial circumstances,[21] or and where the sexual relations indulged in amounted to prostitution,[22] the courts have likewise held that this was sufficient to warrant or be relevant to modification of such a decree.

The courts have also frequently dealt with charges of nonsexual misconduct. One of the charges most frequently involved is the claim that the former wife violated a visitation or custody order; the courts have held such conduct sufficient, if proved, to warrant, or to be relevant to, modification of an order for alimony,[23] although others have held the contrary.[24]

The ex-wife's interference with the former husband's economic interests[25] or her hostile action towards his pres-

9. § 3, infra.

10. § 4[a], infra.

11. § 4[b–d], infra.

12. § 4[c], infra.

13. § 4[d], infra.

14. § 5[a], infra.

15. § 5[b], infra.

16. § 6, infra.

17. § 7, infra.

18. § 8, infra.

19. § 9[a], infra.

20. § 9[b], infra.

21. § 10, infra.

22. § 11, infra.

23. § 12[a], infra.

24. § 12[b], infra.

25. § 13, infra.

Figure 24

ALR INDEX

Consult POCKET PART for Later Annotations

Figure 25

Laches or acquiescence as defense, so as to bar recovery or arrearages of permanent alimony or child support, 5 ALR4th 1015

Spouse's professional decree or license as marital property for purposes of alimony, support, or property settlement, 4 ALR4th 1294

Divorced woman's subsequent sexual relations or misconduct as warranting, alone or with other circumstances, modification of alimony decree, 98 ALR3d 453

Propriety in divorce proceedings of awarding rehabilitative alimony, 97 ALR3d 740

Fault as consideration in alimony, spousal support, or property division awards pursuant to no-fault divorce, 86 ALR3d 1116

Adulterous wife's right to permanent alimony, 86 ALR3d 97

Statute expressly allowing alimony to wife, but not expressly allowing alimony to husband, as unconstitutional sex discrimination, 85 ALR3d 940

Right to allowance of permanent alimony in connection with decree of annulment, 81 ALR3d 281

Divorce: power of court to modify decree for alimony or support of spouse which was based on agreement of parties, 61 ALR3d 520

Wife's possession of independent means as affecting her right to alimony pendente lite, 60 ALR3d 728

Divorce: provision in decree that one party obtain or maintain life insurance for benefit of other party or child, 59 ALR3d 9

Effect of remarriage of spouses to each other on permanent alimony provisions in final divorce decree, 52 ALR3d 1334

Retrospective increase in allowance for alimony, separate maintenance, or support, 52 ALR3d 156

Divorce or separation: consideration of tax liability or consequences in determining alimony or property settlement provisions, 51 ALR3d 461

Valid foreign divorce as affecting local order previously entered for separate maintenance, 49 ALR3d 1266

Annulment of later marriage as reviving prior husband's obligations under alimony decree or separation agreement, 45 ALR3d 1033

Right of child to enforce provisions for his benefit in parents' separation or property settlement agreement, 34 ALR3d 1357

Spouse's acceptance of payments under alimony or property settlement or child support provisions of divorce judgment as precluding appeal therefrom, 29 ALR3d 1184

Court's establishment of trust to secure alimony or child support in divorce proceedings, 3 ALR3d 1170

Propriety and effect of undivided award for support of more than one person, 2 ALR3d 596

Adequacy or excessiveness of amount of money granted as combined award of alimony and child support, 2 ALR3d 537

Adequacy of amount of money awarded as child support (cases since 1946), 1 ALR3d 324

Adequacy or excessiveness of amount of money awarded as temporary alimony (cases since 1946), 1 ALR3d 280

Adequacy or excessiveness of amount of money awarded as separate maintenance, alimony, or support for wife where no absolute divorce is or has been granted, 1 ALR3d 208

Adequacy of amount of money awarded as permanent alimony where divorce is or has been granted (cases since 1946), 1 ALR3d 123

Excessiveness of amount of money awarded as permanent alimony where divorce is or has been granted (cases since 1946), 1 ALR3d 6

Construction and application of 42 USCS § 659(a) authorizing garnishment against United States or District of Columbia for enforcement of child support and alimony obligations, 44 ALR Fed 494

Auto-Cite®: Cases and annotations referred to herein can be further researched through the Auto-Cite® computer-assisted research service. Use Auto-Cite to check citations for form, parallel references, prior and later history, and annotation references.

A statute relating to an allowance from a husband's property to the wife in her action for divorce from bed and board does not create a charge upon the husband's estate or property. *Accardi v Accardi (1964) 97 RI 336, 197 A2d 755, 10 ALR3d 206.*

Payments for separate maintenance become vested when they become due and cannot be modified thereafter. *Porter v Porter (1966) 101 Ariz 131, 416 P2d 564, 34 ALR3d 933, cert den 386 US 957, 18 L Ed 2d 107, 87 S Ct 1028, reh den 386 US 1027, 18 L Ed 2d 472, 87 S Ct 1371.*

That a husband entered into an improvident agreement relating to the amount of alimony is not grounds for relief from a divorce decree incorporating such agreement. *Armstrong v Armstrong (1970) 248 Ark 835, 454 SW2d 660, 61 ALR3d 511.*

[Annotated]

A state statute, which provided that if the wife has not been at fault and has not sufficient means for her support the court may allow her alimony out of the property and earnings of the husband, did not unconstitutionally discriminate against husbands by placing an obligation upon male spouses but no express like obligation upon female spouses. In the absence of a positive legislative statement to the effect that divorced husbands could not claim alimony and in the absence of a case where the husband had been denied or had ever applied for alimony after a divorce, and in view of the fact that alimony for the divorced husband was once available by virtue of a positive state statute,

Figure 26

Vol. 537 **SOUTHERN REPORTER, 2d SERIES (Florida Cases)**

—125—
Henderson v Henderson
1988
s 542So2d989

—129—
Cigna v United Storage Systems Inc.
1988
cc 549So2d252

—130—
Schmitz v S.A.B.T.C. Townhouse Association Inc.
1988
540So2d912
559So2d[1]1161
604So2d1285

—132—
Parham v Reddick
1988
548So2d[5]696

—137—
Lumbermens Mutual Casualty Co. v Florczyk
1988
s 545So2d1367
FCLM§ 19.05

—138—
Keith v Keith
1988
59A3 9s
79A4 22n
79A4 25n
79A4 69n

—140—
Xerographics Inc. v Thomas
1988
545So2d[1]928
e 550So2d564
550So2d[6]565
f 551So2d[1]506
e 551So2d[2]506
f 551So2d[2]506
e 551So2d[3]506
f 551So2d[3]506
e 551So2d[4]506
f 551So2d[4]506
j 551So2d511
f 557So2d[1]940
f 557So2d[2]940
557So2d[4]941
573So2d1028
579So2d133
j 579So2d135
610So2d19
Cir. 5
788FS[1]290
788FS[2]293
Cir. 11
f 874F2d[6]1583
138BRW[1]626
19FSU1115
19FSU1135
41A2 15s
43A2 94s
61A3 397s

—144—
Ferguson v Florida
1989
541So2d[1]1261
550So2d[1]177
571So2d[1]101

—145—
Zubi Advertising Services Inc. v Florida Department of Labor and Unemployment Security
1989
559So2d[1]667

—148—
E.B. v Florida
1989
536So2d[4]372
33A3 798s

—150—
Tarrant v Florida
1989
s 544So2d20
40FlS2d124

—153—
Florida v Jones
1989
r 559So2d1096

—154—
1155 Investment Co. v Tamarac Club Inc.
1989

—155—
Lichtman v Lichtman
1989

—156—
Polk v Crittenden
1989
566So2d[2]1342
571So2d55

—160—
Olenek v Bennett
1989

—162—
Fowler v Unemployment Appeals Commission
1989
s 545So2d1367
d 571So2d[1]1311
1991FlAG98

—164—
Ehrlich v Ehrlich
1989

—165—
Case 1
Knight v Florida
1989

A.L.R. references

—165—
Case 2
Berg v Newton
1989

—168—
School Board of Pinellas County v Smith
1989

—170—
Amazon v Florida
1989
s 547So2d1209
cc 436So2d195
cc 487So2d8
cc 479US914
cc 93LE288
cc 107SC314
559So2d375
578So2d840
Cir. 11
979F2d812

—171—
Case 1
Gray v Crawford
1989
s 542So2d1333

—171—
Case 2
Florida v Hall
1989
557So2d894
566So2d380

—173—
In the Interest of T.D.
1989
s 501So2d93
547So2d[2]984
561So2d359
e 561So2d[3]360
577So2d572
f 580So2d[3]895
j 580So2d896
1A5 565n

—176—
Wilson v Florida
1989

—177—
Reid v Wilson Bottling Corp.
1989

—178—
Florida v Sipe
1989
603So2d65
603So2d[2]65
603So2d[3]65

—180—
Brown v Florida
1989
545So2d446
558So2d[4]545
562So2d[3]696
587So2d[4]661
f 598So2d[4]275
607So2d[4]487
13A5 1240s

—182—
Mrha v Circuit Court for Broward County
1989
50FlS2d62

—185—
McDonald v Florida
1989
576So2d[4]392

—187—
Harris v Florida
1989
576So2d899

—188—
Devoe v Western Auto Supply Co.
1989
576So2d417
59A2 1379s

—190—
Schwartz v Hughes Supply Inc.
1989
583So2d779
30COA449§ 7

—192—
Florida v Davis
1989
cc 538So2d537
544So2d[3]245
554So2d[2]653
557So2d[1]161
579So2d[1]276
581So2d920

—193—
Case 1
Thomas v Florida
1989

—193—
Case 2
Baker v Florida
1989

—194—
Hamilton v Florida
1989
549So2d1129
564So2d[2]165

—195—
Williams v Florida
1989
559So2d[1]609
575So2d754

566

Figure 27

83 ALR SUPPLEMENTAL DECISIONS 272

Aldrich v N. Y. 208 Misc 930, 143 NYS2d 732.
Kingsville Independent School Dist. v. C. (Tex Civ App) 252 SW2d 1022.

83 ALR 1446-1498

Torosian v P. (Ariz) 313 P2d 382 (citing anno).
Krinsky v M. (NH) 128 A2d 915.
Mayo v. M. (Tex Civ App) 269 SW2d 434.

84 ALR 43-100

Supplemented 26 ALR2d 1227.✦

84 ALR 114-117

Hawley v P. C. B. Inc. 345 Mich 500, 76 NW2d 835.
De Luke Ready Mix Corp. v R. — Misc2d —, 161 NYS2d 626.
Rodriguez v J. (Tex Civ App) 289 SW2d 316.

84 ALR 123-129

U. S. v W. M. Corp. (DC Ark) 134 F Supp 898.
Burwell v. P. L. Co. (Miss) 70 So2d 71.

84 ALR 147-165

Selman v. B. (Ala) 72 So2d 704.
Sliman Realty Corp. v. S. E. (La) 73 So2d 447.
Hancock v. C. (Mo App) 267 SW 2d 36.
Appelget v V. H. (NJ Super Ch) 131 A2d 20.
Smith Builders Supply, Inc. v D. (NC) 97 SE2d 767.

84 ALR 180-184

Superseded 1 ALR2d 1101.✦

84 ALR 188-189

Leslie v R. (Kan) 295 P2d 1076.
Gilmore v S. (La App) 79 So2d 192.
Sprong v. P. E. A. (NH) 106 A2d 189.

84 ALR 197-211

J. Ehrlich Realty Co. v D. (Del Ch) 124 A2d 732 (citing anno).
Dietman v H. (Ill) 126 NE2d 22.
Lawrenceville v M. (Ill) 126 NE 2d 671.
Ballard County v. C. S. B. (Ky) 261 SW2d 420.
Board of Equalization v. O. (Ky) 264 SW2d 651.
Anderson Bros. Corp. v S. (Miss) 85 So2d 767.
May Dept. Stores Co. v S. T. C. (Mo) 308 SW2d 748.
Gamboni v O. C. 159 Neb 417, 67 NW2d 489.
Peter Kiewit Sons' Co. v D. C. 161 Neb 93, 72 NW2d 415.
Arlington v C. (Tex) 271 SW2d 414.
Arlington v. C. (Tex Civ App) 263 SW2d 299.

84 ALR 220-249

Snyder v L. V. R. Co. (DC Pa) 143 F Supp 680.
Halada v V. L. P. 132 Cal App2d 788, 283 P2d 42.
Zuber v N. P. R. Co. (Minn) 74 NW2d 641.
Anderson v E. (Neb) 83 NW2d 59.
Guzzi v J. C. P. & L. Co. 36 NJ Super 255, 115 A2d 629.

Re Barnes' Will (App Div) 134 NYS2d 679.
Ackerman v. F. (ND) 54 NW2d 734.
Ross v. T. E. I. Asso. (Tex) 267 SW2d 541.

84 ALR 252-265

Cold Metal Process Co. v R. S. Corp. (CA Ohio) 233 F2d 828.
Kederick v H (DC Alaska) 141 F Supp 633.
Trophy Productions v S. (DC Cal) 17 FRD 416.
Pigg v B. (Idaho) 314 P2d 609.
Shira v C. N. Co. (Nev) 320 P2d 426.
Urquhart v. McE. 204 Misc 426, 126 NYS2d 539.
Grindle v W. F. M. (Sup) 135 NYS2d 21.
Bouche v W. (Or) 293 P2d 203 (citing anno).
Nash v G. (SC) 101 SE2d 283.
Midwest Broadcasting Co. v D. H. Co. (Wis) 78 NW2d 898.

84 ALR 271-278

Superseded 132 ALR 142.✦

84 ALR 281-286

Turner v P. (Idaho) 289 P2d 608.
Barango v E. L. H. C. Co. (Ill App) 138 NE2d 829.
Brandenburg v. B. (Ind App) 114 NE2d 643.
Banberry v. L. (Kan) 244 P2d 202.
Selby v. T. (NM) 249 P2d 498.
Adcox v. A. (NC) 70 SE2d 837.
Smith v S. 98 Ohio App 1, 127 NE2d 637.

84 ALR 294-298

Pacific American Fisheries v. M. (DC Alaska) 108 F Supp 133.
Royal Indem. Co. v B. of E. of M. S. (DC NC) 137 F Supp 890.
Halton Tractor Co. v U. S. (DC Cal) 141 F Supp 411.
Ketchikan Packing Co. v K. (DC Alaska) 130 F Supp 735.
Southern Liquid Gas Co. v. D (Ala) 44 So2d 744.
Title Ins. & Trust Co. v F. T. Bd. 145 Cal App2d 60, 302 P2d 79.
Davis v. C. & C. of D. (Colo) 207 P2d 1185.
Brink v. K. C. (Mo) 221 SW2d 490.
Bucino v. M. 12 NJ 330, 96 A2d 669.
Mercury Mach. Importing Corp. v N. Y. 3 NY2d 418, 165 NYS 2d 517, 144 NE2d 400.
Albert Boris Leasing Corp. v N. Y. (App Div) 136 NYS2d 46.
U. S. Envelope Co. v N. Y. 2 App Div2d 343, 155 NYS2d 816.
Whitehall Pharmacal Co. v N. Y. 10 Misc2d 548, 169 NYS2d 543.
Wampler's Estate (Ohio App) 103 NE2d 303, 60 OL Abs 593.
Sullivan v O. T. C. (Okla) 283 P2d 521 (citing anno).
Central Transp. Co. v A. (Tenn) 305 SW2d 940.
State v A. P. Co. (Tex) 286 SW 2d 110.
State v A. P. Co. (Tex Civ App) 279 SW2d 409.
American Steel & Wire Co. of N. J. v S. 49 Wash2d 419, 302 P2d 207.
Yawkey Bissell Corp. v L. 261 Wis 524, 53 NW2d 174.

84 ALR 299-302

Higgins v. H. (Sup) 119 NYS2d 103.

84 ALR 309-319

Supplemented 156 ALR 1356.✦

84 ALR 324-329

Nagel v T. (Tex Civ App) 275 SW2d 561.
Grindstaff v T. (Tex Civ App) 304 SW2d 270.

84 ALR 337-347

Fowler v. R. (CA DC) 196 F2d 25.
Freeman v F. (Ariz) 291 P2d 795. (citing anno)
People ex rel. Ponak v L. 7 Ill 2d 156, 130 NE2d 190.
Ex parte Grabel (Ky) 248 SW2d 343.
Willin v. S. of W. C. (Md) 95 A 2d 87.
Hayes v. O'C. (Mo App) 263 SW 2d 66.
Thomas v. O'B. (NH) 95 A2d 120.
Ex parte Cohen 12 NJ 362, 96 A2d 794.
Foley v. S. (NJ Super AD) 108 A2d 24.
Ex parte Jackson (Okla Crim App) 262 P2d 722.
Com. ex rel. Heiss v R. 384 Pa 36, 119 A2d 237.
Commonwealth ex rel. Dronsfield v H. (Pa) 135 A2d 757.
Ex parte Quale (Tex Crim App) 298 SW2d 174.
Ex parte Shirley (Tex Crim App) 299 SW2d 701.

84 ALR 355-361

Superseded 143 ALR 548.✦

84 ALR 366-370

Zuber v. Z. 93 Ohio App 195, 112 NE2d 688.

84 ALR 376-378

Dodson v. U. S. (CA Ky) 215 F 2d 196.
Blassingame v U. S. (CA Wash) 220 F2d 25.
Wright v U. S. (CA Ga) 243 F2d 569.

84 ALR 383-386

Woolsley v U. S. (DC NY) 138 F Supp 952.
Connolly v B. of A. N. T. & S. Asso. 138 Cal App2d 303, 291 P2d 501
Re Lanfert's Guardianship (Iowa) 79 NW2d 187 (citing anno).
Harrell v W. (Ky) 283 SW2d 197.
Coughlin v. C. (Mass) 94 A2d 79.
Dillard v. T. (Mo App) 270 SW 2d 548.
Schroeder v E. 161 Neb 252, 73 NW2d 165.
Guerin v C. 38 NJ Super 454, 119 A2d 780.
Re Russell's Estate (Pa) 123 A2d 708 (citing anno).

84 ALR 389-390

Green v P. O. S. of A. 242 NC 78, 87 SE2d 14.

84 ALR 393-403

Tomlinson v O. G. & E. Co. (Okla) 305 P2d 521.
Wilson v. K. (Or) 258 P2d 112.

✦When Supplemented see later Note and Blue Book under caption of later Note

Figure 28

paper articles in question were of purely informational nature, did not refer to defendant's case, and were not type of news articles that would reasonably be expected to create prejudice against this particular defendant. State v Spraggin, 71 Wis 2d 604, 239 NW2d 297.

15 ALR2d 1158–1160

Relative priority, in bankruptcy reorganization proceeding, as between judgment against debtor for personal injuries to, or death of, one other than employee, and pre-existing mortgage covering debtor's property.

Construction and application of § 116(1) of Bankruptcy Act (11 USCS § 516(1)), authorizing court to permit rejection of executory contracts of debtor in Chapter X reorganization proceedings. 34 ALR Fed 743.

VERALEX™: Cases and annotations referred to herein can be further researched through the VERALEX electronic retrieval system's two services, **Auto-Cite®** and **SHOWME™**. Use Auto-Cite to check citations for form, parallel references, prior and later history, and annotation references. Use SHOWME to display the full text of cases and annotations.

Debt owed plaintiff corporation would not be dischargeable in bankruptcy, notwithstanding debtor's allegation he and plaintiff were in partnership in travel business, and therefore he was not in fiduciary relationship with plaintiff, in light of evidence sufficient to support finding that debtor embezzled within meaning of bankruptcy statute. Funventures in Travel, Inc. v Dunn (1984, ED Pa) 39 BR 249.

15 ALR2d 1165–1193

Guest's knowledge that automobile driver has been drinking as precluding recovery, under guest statutes or equivalent common-law rule

§ 1. Scope, p. 1167.

Physical defect, illness, drowsiness, or falling asleep of motor vehicle operator as affecting liability for injury. 28 ALR2d 12.

Comment Note.—Distinction between assumption of risk and contributory negligence. 82 ALR2d 1218.

Liability for injury to or death of passenger from accident due to physical condition of carrier's employee. 52 ALR3d 669.

Motor vehicle passenger's contributory negligence or assumption of risk where accident resulted from driver's drowsiness, physical defect, or illness. 1 ALR4th 556.

Evidence of automobile passenger's blood alcohol level as admissible in support of defense that passenger was contributorily negligent or assumed risk of automobile accident. 5 ALR4th 1194.

Answers—Affirmative defenses—Contributory negligence—Participation in activities leading to intoxication of driver. 3 Am Jur Pl & Pr Forms (Rev ed), Automobiles and Highway Traffic, Form 1353.

Complaint—Condition and status of driver —Intoxication—Speeding—Weaving Plaintiff thrown from automobile. 3 Am Jur Pl & Pr Forms (Rev ed), Automobiles and Highway Traffic, Form 413.

Instructions—Contributory negligence—Riding with intoxicated driver. 3 Am Jur Pl & Pr Forms (Rev ed), Automobiles and Highway Traffic, Form 1623.

Instructions—Occupants of vehicles—Guest statutes—Definition under gift statute—"Intoxication." 3 Am Jur Pl & Pr Forms (Rev ed), Automobiles and Highway Traffic, Form 1612.

Guest riding with intoxicated driver. 2 Am Jur Proof of Facts, Assumption of Risk, Proof 2.

16 Am Jur Proof of Facts 569, Alcoholism.

22 Am Jur Proof of Facts 123, Physical Disabilities of Motor Vehicle Drivers—Vision and Hearing Defects.

Contributory negligence of passenger accepting ride with driver suffering from drowsiness, illness, or physical defects. 20 Am Jur Proof of Facts 2d 667

VERALEX™: Cases and annotations referred to herein can be further researched through the VERALEX electronic retrieval system's two services, **Auto-Cite®** and **SHOWME™**. Use Auto-Cite to check citations for form, parallel references, prior and later history, and annotation references. Use SHOWME to display the full text of cases and annotations.

§ 3. Generally, p. 1167.

Recognizing general rule that knowledge may preclude recovery:

Ark—Poole v James (Ark) 332 SW2d 833.

Cal—See Enos v Montoya, 158 Cal App 2d 394, 322 P2d 472; Bradbeer v Scott, 193 Cal App 2d 575, 14 Cal Rptr 458; Cowan v Bunce, 212 Cal App 2d 48, 27 Cal Rptr 758; Godinez v Soares, 216 Cal App 2d 145, 30 Cal Rptr 767;

Figure 29

ALR TABLES

37 ALR4th 10
§ 4 Superseded 74 ALR5th 319

37 ALR4th 382
Superseded 14 ALR5th 695

38 ALR4th 628
Superseded 83 ALR5th 467

38 ALR4th 1219
Superseded 52 ALR5th 195

44 ALR4th 595
Superseded 88 ALR5th 1

51 ALR4th 872
Superseded 88 ALR5th 301

56 ALR4th 375
Superseded 74 ALR5th 1

57 ALR4th 911
§ 3, 7[a] Superseded 98 ALR Fed 124

58 ALR4th 76
§ 18 Superseded 69 ALR5th 137

62 ALR4th 758
Superseded 71 ALR5th 307

69 ALR4th 1127
Superseded 76 ALR5th 289

71 ALR4th 305
§ 3, 4 Superseded 82 ALR5th 443
83 ALR5th 375
84 ALR5th 191

78 ALR4th 435
Superseded 81 ALR5th 367

82 ALR4th 26
§ 14-16 Superseded 77 ALR5th 595

90 ALR4th 586
Superseded 72 ALR5th 403

ALR5th

14 ALR5th 242
§ 48 Superseded 86 ALR5th 397

44 ALR5th 393
§ 13 Superseded 79 ALR5th 409

ALR Fed

1 ALR Fed 295
Superseded 105 ALR Fed 755

1 ALR Fed 370
Superseded 111 ALR Fed 295

1 ALR Fed 395
§ 4[b], 6[b], 7[b] Superseded 67 ALR Fed 463

1 ALR Fed 519
§ 4 Superseded 60 ALR Fed 204

1 ALR Fed 719
123 ALR Fed 203

1 ALR Fed 838
§ 10 Superseded 69 ALR Fed 251

1 ALR Fed 965
Superseded 56 ALR Fed 326

1 ALR Fed 1020
Superseded 111 ALR Fed 83

2 ALR Fed 180
§ 11 Superseded 114 ALR Fed 551

2 ALR Fed 347
Superseded 129 ALR Fed 273

2 ALR Fed 545
Superseded 141 ALR Fed 445

2 ALR Fed 811
Superseded 134 ALR Fed 257

2 ALR Fed 978
Superseded 147 ALR Fed 613

3 ALR Fed 29
§ 15[c] Superseded 125 ALR Fed 1

3 ALR Fed 592
Superseded 134 ALR Fed 289

3 ALR Fed 843
§ 4 Superseded 127 ALR Fed 141
§ 9 Superseded 129 ALR Fed 377
129 ALR Fed 343
133 ALR Fed 229

4 ALR Fed 343
Superseded 92 ALR Fed 333

4 ALR Fed 723
§ 4-10 Superseded 167 ALR Fed 1
§ 11 Superseded 30 ALR Fed 421

4 ALR Fed 1048
§ 12 Superseded 59 ALR Fed 10

5 ALR Fed 246
§ 18 Superseded 133 ALR Fed 549

5 ALR Fed 440
§ 9 Superseded 30 ALR Fed 421

5 ALR Fed 518
§ 4(q) Superseded 132 ALR Fed 147

5 ALR Fed 674
§ 13-15 Superseded 92 ALR Fed 733

6 ALR Fed 906
§ 4, 5 Superseded 120 ALR Fed 145

7 ALR Fed 110
§ 4[b], 6[b] Superseded 67 ALR Fed 463

7 ALR Fed 855
Superseded 168 ALR Fed 143

7 ALR Fed 950
§ 3 Superseded 106 ALR Fed 33

8 ALR Fed 550
§ 5 Superseded 67 ALR Fed 463

8 ALR Fed 675
§ 2.5, 3 Superseded 97 ALR Fed 369
§ 4-6 Superseded 139 ALR Fed 553

9 ALR Fed 16
§ 12 Superseded 30 ALR Fed 421

9 ALR Fed 685
Superseded 26 ALR5th 628

10 ALR Fed 185
§ 3-5 Superseded 119 ALR Fed 589
§ 6, 7 Superseded 115 ALR Fed 381

10 ALR Fed 844
Superseded 109 ALR Fed 488

10 ALR Fed 940
Superseded 111 ALR Fed 235

11 ALR Fed 316
§ 9, 11 Superseded 149 ALR Fed 431

11 ALR Fed 713
§ 1-5, 7, 8 Superseded 110 ALR Fed 626

11 ALR Fed 786
§ 1-4, 6, 6.5, 8 Superseded 117 ALR Fed 515

11 ALR Fed 815
§ 4 Superseded 113 ALR Fed 173

12 ALR Fed 15
§ 8 Superseded 123 ALR Fed 1

Consult POCKET PART for Later Entries

Computerized Databases

Libraries are no different than the rest of the world—they are becoming increasingly computerized. In fact, libraries are often at the forefront of computerization. In the not-so-distant past, you would have to wait weeks for information that was not available on the library shelves because a librarian would have to order it for you from another *lending library*. The lending library would then mail the materials to your library, which would call you to pick up the materials. Now, vast amounts of information are available almost instantaneously. A librarian in any city in the country can contact New York, Los Angeles, even London or Beijing, and obtain information that is then either captured on disk or printed out for you.

CD-ROM

In addition to the various online information networks available to libraries, librarians make a great deal of use of CD-ROM products. Even in the most rural of communities, everything from the old card catalog to encyclopedias is housed on CD-ROMs.

It makes sense for libraries—especially law libraries—to be computerized. Just consider what you read in Chapter 4 on case research.

Reporters take up an enormous amount of space. One compact disc can hold about two-hundred thousand pages of text-only information. In lieu of succumbing to the information explosion by building a new, larger facility every five years, a library can install a few more CD-ROM multimedia terminals instead. They are a highly cost-effective way to deliver vast amounts of information without taking up large amounts of space. By and large, they are easy to use.

CD-ROM is the abbreviated version of *Compact Disc—Read Only Memory*. This means that the information may only be read and may not be altered by the user. No matter how you attempt to enter information, none of it will be permanently added to the information on the disc. The information on a CD-ROM may be text-only, pictures- or graphics-only, or may be a combination of text and graphics. Some have music, speech, or other sound effects. Others have movies and other video capabilities.

As discussed, a CD-ROM has an immense capacity—over two-hundred thousand pages of information if the data is text-only. Think of how many pages the average book contains. The average case reporter contains between eight hundred and one thousand pages. It would be possible, then, for two hundred volumes of reporters to be placed on one CD-ROM. Think of how much space a compact disc takes up compared to the space one book takes up, let alone an entire set of books. You can begin to see that libraries, regardless of size, are at a tremendous advantage using CD-ROMs.

Each CD-ROM has its own search technique, which makes it impossible for this book to show you how to formulate searches. Do not let this discourage you. CD-ROM products today are user-friendly. Most give you total on-screen support with a wide range of instructions and help screens. If all else fails and you cannot figure it out, ask a librarian for help.

In recent years, the CD-ROM format has been successfully challenged by use of the Internet and expanded computer assisted legal research databases. Although some law firms and libraries may continue to selectively utilize CD-ROM products, the great majority have switched to online databases and the Internet. (see Chapter 8.)

WESTLAW AND LEXISNEXIS

Both *Westlaw* and *LexisNexis* are online legal databases, also called *computer-assisted legal research* or CALR. *Westlaw* is provided by Thomson West, and is based in Eagan, Minnesota. *LexisNexis* is provided by Reed Elsevier Inc., and is based in Dayton, Ohio. Both systems are geared almost exclusively to legal professionals and law students. The online libraries are extensive. They cover everything from cases and statutes to law reviews.

Both databases require passwords to access the system. A lawyer may have a password if he or she has a contract and pays the monthly fee. Probably the most active users of Westlaw and LexisNexis are law students. Both companies provide passwords to each student, professor, and librarian for virtually every law school in the country. The students are trained to use both databases, and they generally have unlimited access while in school. Their passwords are deactivated once they graduate.

Each database has its own search terminology that includes both a type of boolean logic and a *natural language* algorithm, and requires instruction for use—more instruction than can be disseminated in this book. This is one important reason that access is usually restricted. The other reason is that it is much more practical when a lawyer's client is being charged for research time. The average cost of using one of these databases is between four and six dollars per minute. An experienced searcher can save a lawyer's client a great deal of money.

A good online search may take twenty or thirty minutes, costing approximately $150.00, while the same research done by using books may take two or three hours, costing anywhere from $150.00 to $500.00 (depending upon whether the law firm is charging for an attorney's time, paralegal's time, or even a law clerk's time, which is a law student working at a firm).

Staying online for hours, however, is usually unproductive. *Westlaw* and *LexisNexis* are prohibitively expensive unless you know what you are looking for with a reasonable degree of certainty. Their greatest asset is speed, and for that you must know how to do an effective online search. It is important to note that even someone who has trained on either *Westlaw* or *LexisNexis* (or both) will not be a good online researcher unless he or she becomes a good book researcher first.

While there are other online databases, including *Loislaw* and *Versuslaw*, all of them require subscriptions that are often cost-prohibitive for the average consumer. If you really need information from one of these databases, confer with the librarian. Librarians often have access to these databases and will perform searches as a courtesy to library patrons. Another avenue is to use the Internet, which is the subject of the next chapter.

Legal Research on the Internet

chapter 8

From what you have read in prior chapters, the legal community has developed a very precise method of finding legal materials. If you follow the rules, you have a much greater chance of finding the answer to your question. Although potentially expensive to purchase, CALR and CD-ROM can be quite precise. In fact, despite the need for search queries, both CALR and CD-ROM use the traditional legal research framework.

Enter the *Internet*—for a low monthly fee (and sometimes free), you can search the globe for legal materials. Until a few years ago, finding legal information on the Internet was a daunting task. The Internet was wild and confusing. Most sites with legal information were not indexed in any fashion. Searching for anything specific could be like looking for the proverbial needle in a haystack. Luckily, this has changed.

In the recent past, much of the Internet's available legal sources have been vastly improved, making them much more accessible. A plethora of websites are available, and detailed search engines make finding the materials easy and fast. What makes this form of research even better is that much of it is absolutely free. This chapter introduces you to some of the best legal sites on the Internet.

FINDING RESOURCES ON THE INTERNET USING SEARCH ENGINES

A *search engine* is a program that will allow you to search the Web for websites that match the information you specify in a *query*, or question. Search engines are necessary because if you use a good search query, they will provide you with a wealth of good information. Otherwise, you will have to hunt and peck your way through the Internet, and if that is not a completely impossible task, it is tremendously time-consuming.

That is not to say that a good query will always yield excellent results. It will not. Search engines often provide what can only be called *garbage*, as well as good information. This is the frustrating aspect of using search engines. What you think is a good, tight query might yield ten thousand or more results, many of which have absolutely nothing to do with what you need. Some search engines will find personal homepages as well as serious research websites. Others find websites that are merely advertisements for consumer and business products. Some find both.

Anyone who uses the Internet for any length of time develops a preference for which search engine to use. Ask your friends and colleagues which search engines they prefer, and get the addresses from them. You might find an engine you have never heard of before.

Another method is to click on the search link in whatever Internet browser (i.e., *Internet Explorer*, *Firefox*, *Netscape*, etc.) you use. Doing this will take you to a Web page that will allow you to enter a search query.

Following is a list of common Internet search engines and their URLs. What is most important is that on the Internet, sites come and go rather quickly, so if you cannot connect to a site because you get a *site not available* or *site not found* message, the site may have been moved or may no longer exist. It happens. Just move on to your next choice.

GENERAL SEARCH ENGINES
(in no particular order)

Google:	www.google.com
Alta Vista:	www.altavista.com
Dogpile:	www.dogpile.com
Lycos:	www.lycos.com
Yahoo:	www.yahoo.com
Hotbot (part of the Lycos family):	www.hotbot.com
Metacrawler:	www.metacrawler.com
Mamma:	www.mamma.com

LEGAL SEARCH ENGINES:
(in alphabetical order)

Detod:	www.detod.com
Law & Policy Institutions Guide:	www.lpig.org
Law Crawler:	http://lawcrawler.findlaw.com
Legal Engine:	www.legalengine.com
Law Guru:	www.lawguru.com/search/lawsearch.html
LawKt.com:	http://news.surfwax.com/law
Law Runner:	www.ilrg.com/gov.html
LegalTrek:	www.legaltrek.com

FINDING LEGAL RESOURCES ON THE WEB

As previously stated, finding legal resources on the Web has become much easier. The first reason for this is the increase in the number of legal websites. Some of these sites are inclusive—that is, they provide the information directly on that Web page. Other sites act as legal search engines. Plug in the information you require, and the site's search engine will connect you to the proper legal Web page in the blink of an eye. This is a particularly nice feature because you will not have to keep track of every legal site you find. Just keep track of the legal search engine information and let it do the rest for you.

The second reason is that the individual websites have refined their searching techniques. At one time, if you wanted to find a Supreme Court case, you had to literally hunt and peck for it. Now, some sites allow you to find it by volume and page, case name, and even keyword search. This is a vast improvement. In fact, many legal sites now provide for keyword search, a vital tool for finding anything using a computer.

The third reason for the improvements in finding legal research on the Internet has to do with the increase in the information available. The increase has been enormous. For example, you can now access United States Supreme Court cases back to the 1800s. You can find state statutes online and up-to-date. No need to trudge to a law library, and no need to pay for CD-ROM or CALR.

Another wonderful point about using the Internet for finding legal resources is that you can save all of it immediately to your computer's hard drive or to a disk, and access it when it is convenient for you. No need to print it immediately.

Following are some legal websites, as well as other Internet sites with access to legal information. The list is far from exhaustive. Keep in mind that the Internet changes on a daily basis and that a website that is available one day may be gone the next.

Two of the best legal online sites are **www.findlaw.com** and the Cornell Law School Legal Information Institute (LII) at **www.law.cornell.edu**. A state's own official site generally will provide access to its laws (statutes or code) and sometimes even cases.

To find federal cases and codes:

http://findlaw.com/casecode
www4.law.cornell.edu/uscode

To find state cases and codes (index pages):

http://findlaw.com/casecode/state.html
www.law.cornell.edu/states/listing.html

Other Sites:

Catalaw:	www.catalaw.com
Law.com:	www.law.com
US Law:	www.uslaw.com
FedWorld:	www.fedworld.gov
Federal Judicial Center:	www.fjc.gov
Federal Web Locator:	www.infoctr.edu/fwl
State Web Locator:	www.infoctr.edu/swl
Fed Law:	www.thecre.com/fedlaw/default.htm
Library of Congress:	www.loc.gov
American Bar Association:	www.abanet.org
Internet Legal Research Group:	www.ilrg.com
US Courts:	www.uscourts.gov
LawGuru:	www.lawguru.com

NOTE: *Pick a law school and you will probably find an online library.*

For a list of all American Bar Association approved law schools (with their websites), see **www.abanet.org/legaled/approvedlawschools/alpha.html**.

Putting It All Together

chapter 9

Now that you have been introduced to the world of legal research, it is time for you to put all your newfound skills together. You may notice that all the different methods fit together like a puzzle. One piece may not make much sense by itself, but put them all together and you have a beautiful picture—the answer to your legal problem.

ASK A LIBRARIAN

As discussed in Chapter 1, a law librarian can be very helpful. In most libraries, a law librarian has been through college and also has either a master's degree in Library of Science or a law degree. Many have both, which is fast becoming a requirement for the job.

What does this mean to you? It means that the librarian is going to know where to find the materials you require. More importantly, it means the librarian is going to know how to do legal research and will understand your problem. You will be able to ask questions about your legal situation and not get a blank stare.

However, it does not mean you can solicit legal advice. Even if the librarian is a lawyer, he or she will probably be prohibited from giving you any legal advice. The librarian will be happy to help you find the materials, but you will be on your own when it comes time to interpret them.

Reading this book will help you to have a basic understanding of the system before you ask for assistance. You should try to do as much research as you can without asking for help. First, you will learn how to use the materials better if you do so. Second, as discussed in Chapter 1, many libraries have limited reference help for people outside the legal community. This is especially true of law school libraries, which are geared to the needs of the students and professors.

That does not mean they will not help you. It simply means that the librarian cannot spend hours assisting you with research, so anything you accomplish before asking for help is to your benefit. Just remember that a little sweat is good, but if you find you are being driven to tears, it is time to call in the cavalry. Ask the librarian.

WHEN ENOUGH IS ENOUGH

How do you know when you are through researching? This is mostly a subjective matter. Do you think you have enough materials to support your argument? If you have all the statutes and cases you could find, if you collected a few A.L.R. annotations, a law review article or two, and quotes from a treatise, you may be a victim of overkill.

Face it, if you find a brand-new case that is 100% on point with your problem, you are in great shape, but those cases are hard to find. Usually, you are in good shape if you can show, either through statutes, cases, or both, that your situation is supported over time. In general, if you can accumulate a dozen cases or so, and maybe a statute to support your position, you have done plenty.

On the other hand, there are times when no matter how long you look, no matter where you look, and no matter how much assistance you garner, you will not find anything. Do not panic. It happens. If you have searched high and low and in every nook and cranny in the library, and cannot find anything to support your situation, you may have an issue that has never been discussed before. This is your answer. You have done everything possible. Go home, and call a lawyer in the morning.

If you really think it is necessary, you may want to ask the librarian to help you reframe your ideas. That may get you onto another track that is more fruitful. If that does not work, or if you already did that and still came up empty-handed, give up, go home, have some dinner, and get a good night's sleep. Then, think about calling a lawyer.

SUMMARY OF STEPS FOR EFFECTIVE LEGAL RESEARCH

The following twelve steps will help you assess what your legal problem is and how you can solve it.

1. Determine what your problem is. Come up with a question that accurately frames the situation. For example, if you want alimony from your spouse, you might ask yourself the following questions.

    - What are the requirements for alimony in my state?
    - How much money am I entitled to?
    - How long may I receive alimony?
    - May I still collect alimony if I have remarried?

2. Think up all the possible words to help describe your situation.

3. See if your library has a self-help book, practice manual, legal encyclopedia, or treatise on the area of law you need to research. If so, get it and see if you can find your answer there. This is also a good thing to do if you are not sure of the issue you need to research.

4. Think about whether there is, or may be, a statute pertaining to your question. Depending on the situation, you will then use either a statute (to find a particular law or find cases relating to a particular law) or a digest (to find cases). If there is a statute, it may either answer your question or its annotations may lead you to the cases you need. You may also want to look up cases separately in a digest.

5. To look up statutes, use the index and find any statutes pertaining to your problem. Read them. Make sure they are up-to-date. Make a note of cases you find in the annotations to the statutes that sound helpful.

6. To look for cases without the statutes, go to the digest and find citations for every case that may be helpful to your situation.

7. Look up the cases in the reporters. Read them. Separate the good ones you might use from the bad ones you do not, and discard the latter.

8. Make note of any headnotes that seem particularly helpful. Also, note any additional topics and key number headings that may be of assistance to you.

9. Shepardize the good cases, paying close attention to the cases referring to the headnotes you noted.

10. Read the cases you just obtained through *Shepard's*. Separate the good ones from the bad ones, discard the bad ones, and shepardize the good ones. After a while, you may have a pile of helpful cases. Only you will be able to determine when to stop reading, shepardizing, reading, shepardizing, etc. If there are no citations in Shepard's, you are definitely finished with case research. Also, shepardize any statutes you may have found.

11. Trouble finding anything? Remember A.L.R. Remember treatises and monographs. Remember law reviews.

12. Remember to ask librarians if you need help finding materials and that using a computer may help speed up all of these steps.

Glossary

A

advance sheets. Supplemental pamphlets that add new case opinions to reporters.

A.L.R. *See American Law Reports.*

American Jurisprudence 2d. A legal encyclopedia covering the laws of all fifty states and the federal government.

American Law Reports (A.L.R.). A set of books that report on legal topics of general interest. *See also annotations.*

Am Jur. *See American Jurisprudence 2d.*

annotations. (1) Abstracts, or summaries, of cases construing a particular point of law. (2) Comprehensive legal writings found in *American Law Reports*.

appellate court. A court that hears appeals from trial courts.

argument. Remarks or oral presentation made in court by attorneys on behalf of the parties involved.

B

bill. A proposal for a law.

burden of proof. The responsibility of producing enough evidence to support the issues in a lawsuit, so as to persuade the judge or jury in your favor.

C

case law. The written opinions of judges in particular lawsuits.

case opinions. *See case law.*

citation. The way all legal materials are quoted. It is a form of legal shorthand used to give information about where a case or statute can be found.

cited case. The case you are shepardizing. *See Shepard's Citations.*

citing case. The case that refers to the one you are shepardizing. *See Shepard's Citations.*

claimant. Someone who believes he or she has a claim against another.

compact disc. A computer disc that is capable of storing large quantities of information.

constructive service of process. The act of notifying a person that he or she is being sued by placing a notice in the newspaper and mailing him or her a copy.

contempt of court. An act that hinders a court in its attempt to carry out the law.

Corpus Juris Secundum (CJS). A legal encyclopedia covering the laws of all fifty states and the federal government.

court opinion. *See opinion.*

creditor. Someone who is owed money. The debt may be based upon an agreement to pay or upon a court order to pay.

Current Law Index. A guide to locating law reviews and legal periodicals.

D

debtor. A person who owes money to another.

decennial digests (decennials). Sets of digests, grouped in ten year periods, which cover all of the states and all federal jurisdictions.

defendant. A person against whom a lawsuit is filed.

deposition. Testimony (outside of court) under oath, which may be taken down in writing.

digest. The primary guide to finding case law in reporters. It is a compilation of abstracts or summaries of each case in a particular jurisdiction or legal area.

due process. A concept that each person must be treated fairly by the government. The interpretation of this concept changes depending upon the interpretation of the judge. Ultimately, the United States Supreme Court decides what process is due, but this can also change from term to term.

E

en banc. When all of an appellate court's judges sit in on an argument. It means *on the bench* or *full bench*.

G

garnish. To order a third party to turn over to a creditor any property that is being held for a debtor.

grantee. A person who received property from another.

grantor. A person who transfers property to another.

H

headnote. A brief summary of a legal rule or significant fact in a case.

I

index. An alphabetical listing of subject references with their location in a book or set of books.

Index to Legal Periodicals. A guide to law reviews and legal periodicals.

Internet. Connection of computers allowing for an exchange of information.

Internet service provider (ISP). An Internet host, which is necessary to gain access to the Internet. Hosts often charge a fee for access.

J

judgment. A court document announcing the outcome of a case, often declaring that a sum of money is owed.

judgment debtor. A person who owes money, the amount of which has been decided by the court in the form of a judgment.

K

key number. A method of linking cases on the same point and so you can search legal issues by concepts (only West Publishing has key numbers).

L

law reviews. Journals published by law schools.

legal periodicals. Law-related journals and newsletters that are not classified as law reviews.

LegalTrac. A CD-ROM method for locating law reviews and legal periodicals.

levy. Seizure of property by a sheriff. The property may be physically taken or left in place with a notice posted on or near it.

LexisNexis. An online legal database.

M

modem. The equipment that creates the telephone link between computers.

monographs. Books that only cover a very small portion of a subject.

N

notice. Notification of a claim or lawsuit.

O

on all fours. A case that is identical to your case in every way.

online. The link between computers over telephone lines.

online database. A source of information accessed through a telephone connection.

opinion. The written decision of a court.

P

perjury. False testimony given under oath. Perjury is a crime.

plaintiff. A person who files a lawsuit.

pocket part. A small pamphlet placed in a slat or pocket in a book, meant as an update in lieu of printing a new hardbound book.

precedent. A court's opinion furnishing an example, or authority, for an identical or similar case based on a similar question of law.

R

regulations. Rules that are promulgated, or declared, by a state or federal agency.

reporters. Books in which case law is published.

Roget's. A thesaurus that provides a list of synonyms and antonyms for the word you are looking up.

S

search engine. Computer program that enables a person to find information, especially websites, on the Internet.

service of process. The delivery of court papers to a person, giving notification that a court action has been commenced against him or her.

Shepard's Citations. A guide to determining if cases and statutes are still valid law and for finding other sources related to them.

shepardizing. The act of using *Shepard's Citations*.

subpoena. An order by a court to appear or to produce something at a court hearing, deposition, etc.

summons. A notice by a court that a lawsuit has been filed.

T

topic and key number. A word, phrase, or abbreviation, in boldface type, and a number, to which a digest refers you instead of a page number.

treatises. Books that cover an entire field of law.

trial. Courtroom proceeding which determines the outcome of a lawsuit.

trust. An arrangement whereby one person (the trustee) holds property for another person or persons (the beneficiary).

trustee. A person who holds property for another under a trust arrangement.

W

Web browser. Software that enables a person to read information on the World Wide Web.

Web page. One page on the Internet. A group of Web pages will comprise a website.

website. Where information is found on the World Wide Web, or Internet.

World Wide Web. A popular method of accessing information on the Internet.

Westlaw. An online legal database that provides access to entire libraries of legal information.

Sample Research Problem

appendix

This appendix is an example of a research problem. It will give you an idea of how to conduct legal research. This exercise will not give you an answer to the problem. It is only a guide—something to show you the possible steps for a particular type of problem. These steps are fairly universal, however, and you can rely on them to help you with your own problem. The research was conducted for Florida. Research tools are common to all states and this research can be duplicated for any of them.

NOTE: *The symbol § means "section," as in the section number of a statute.*

THE PROBLEM

You visit Go-Mart, your local grocery store, after work to pick up a few items for dinner. While walking past the produce section, you slip on a grape. You not only injured your pride, you also broke your coccyx (tailbone), which required surgery. Now you want to sue Go-Mart for your injuries, and you need to know whether Go-Mart can be held responsible.

Do you need to prove what caused you to slip and fall? Does it make a difference if a store's employees knew the grape was there? These are just two of many questions you may need to answer before filing suit. Of course, you should first get an overview of the particular area of law, so you can find out what the important questions are.

FLORIDA RESEARCH

As always, it is important to think about all possible words describing the problem. Some words applicable to this problem are slip (slipped, slipping, slippery); slipping and falling (slip and fall); negligence; injury; and, liability.

Encyclopedia

When you do not know much about the subject or are unsure of terminology, it is wise to start in a legal encyclopedia (unless you can find a practice manual). *Florida Jurisprudence 2d* (Fla.Jur.2d) is the legal encyclopedia to use for Florida research.

Beginning in the general index, you would find a listing for "Slip and fall." The topic "Slip and fall" refers you to "Premises Liability." Under "Premises Liability," you will find "Slip and fall cases" with a subheading for "notice or knowledge of condition, duty to maintain safe conditions for invitees, Premises §32, 33." (See Figure A, page 149.)

Look for the volume with the section titled "Premises Liability" and turn to Section 33. Section 33 is a checklist for foreign substance cases. (see Figure B, page 150). Not only does this section of the encyclopedia list what you will need to prove the case, it tells you that the pertinent case digest section is Negligence, key number 1095. Remember to check the pocket part inside the back cover of the volume for the most recent information.

Digest

You already know that one important digest topic is Negligence 1095, but explore the digests regardless.

NOTE: *One case relating to the general topic of slip and fall cases under "Negligence 1095" is shown in Figure D1 for illustration purposes.*

Since you know now that it is a good place to start, look under "Premises Liability" in the general index first. Under "Premises Liability" are a few entries under "Slips and falls in general." One that stands out is a subheading of "Floors," which is Neglig 1104(3). (see Figure C, page 151). If you are unfamiliar with the topic abbreviation, check the front of the volume for a list of topics and their abbreviations. "Neglig" means Negligence.

Find the volume containing "Negligence" and advance to key number 1104(3). To get the most recent cases, be sure to look in the pocket part inside the back cover of the book. Looking in *Florida Digest, 2d,* however, there are no cases corresponding. (see Figure D1, page 152.) This happens, as the digest topics will often be the same for each state's digest. A casual glance, however, shows that under Negligence 1104(7), which is a related topic, there is a case summary concerning a nursing home visitor that slipped on a grape while visiting a resident. (see Figure D2, page 153.) The case is Markowitz v. Helen Homes of Kendall Corp., 736 So.2d 775.

Reporter

If you want to see exactly what the appellate court said, you will need to look up the case in the reporter. (see Figure E, page 154.)

Shepard's

Remember to follow the instructions for *Shepard's* in Chapter 5 carefully. You must look in each volume of Shepard's containing your case. The newer the case, the less likely another court will have cited it. Markowitz is a 1999 case. To shepardize that case, first locate the Shepard's for the *Southern Reporter, 2d Series*. Next, find the page that says "Vol. 736" in the upper corner. Finally, locate the page number, which is "—775—." Under that listing you will find one case, to be found at 788 So.2d 286. (see Figure F, page 156.)

Statutes

The first place to begin a search for statutes is the index. Look up all the words you think apply in Florida Statutes or Florida Statutes Annotated.

Once you have begun the task, you may begin to feel frustrated because no matter what word or word combinations you look up, you cannot find statutes pertaining to slip and fall cases. What is the answer? There is none. In Florida, laws pertaining to slip and fall type negligence actions are not statutory. You must rely on case law.

§ 33 —Checklist for foreign substance cases

Research References

West's Key Number Digest, Negligence ⚷1095

The following facts and circumstances, among others, tend to establish that the operator of a commercial enterprise is liable to a person who slipped and fell due, allegedly, to the presence of a foreign substance on the floor of the premises (note that not all of these facts and circumstances will exist in any given case; the applicability of some of them will depend, of course, on the theory on which the alleged negligence is based):[1]

- existence of duty owed by defendant to plaintiff
  - — plaintiff's status as business invitee
  - — duty of reasonable care under circumstances, regardless of plaintiff's status
- plaintiff's slip and fall on floor of premises
- existence of hazardous condition
  - — presence of foreign substance on floor at place and time of accident
  - — description and identification of foreign substance
  - — slipperiness of floor
  - — presence of foreign substance on plaintiff's body or clothing after accident
- nature of foreign substance
  - — product sold by defendant or related to its business
  - — area closed to public as source of substance
  - — defendant's equipment as source of substance

[Section 33]

[1]Am. Jur. 2d, Premises Liability §§ 554 to 614.

Forms References: For personal injuries from slip and fall on oily substance. Florida Pleading and Practice Forms (Rev), Torts § 28:20.

and fall case. Slip and Fall Due to Foreign Substance on Floor, 28 Am. Jur. Proof of Facts 2d 167 §§ 19 to 41.

Existence of dangerous condition arising from improper maintenance of floor. Slip and Fall, 10 Am. Jur. Proof of Facts 785, proof 1.

References are to Digest Topics and Key Numbers

PREMISES LIABILITY—Cont'd

PROXIMATE cause. See heading
PROXIMATE CAUSE, PREMISES
liability.

PUBLIC amusements. See heading
THEATERS AND SHOWS, generally.

PUBLIC invitee, **Neglig** ☞ 1037(5)

PURCHASERS,
Parties liable, **Neglig** ☞ 1264

RAMPS,
Breach of duty. See subheading STAIRS
and ramps, under this heading.

REASONABLE care standard, **Neglig**
☞ 1032

REASONABLY safe condition,
Standard of care, **Neglig** ☞ 1033

RECREATIONAL use doctrine and statutes,
Generally, **Neglig** ☞ 1191-1197
Construction of statutes in general, **Neglig**
☞ 1193
Duty of care, **Neglig** ☞ 1196
Fee or charge for use, **Neglig** ☞ 1195
Persons covered by doctrine, **Neglig**
☞ 1194
Property,
Activities and conditions covered by
doctrine, **Neglig** ☞ 1194
Purpose of doctrine, **Neglig** ☞ 1192
Standard of care, **Neglig** ☞ 1196
Warning, **Neglig** ☞ 1196
Willful or malicious acts, **Neglig** ☞ 1197

REGULATORY requirements. See subheading STATUTORY requirements, under
this heading.

RELIGIOUS societies, **Relig Soc** ☞ 30

REPAIRS. See subheading
CONSTRUCTION, demolition and
repairs, under this heading.

RES ipsa loquitur, **Neglig** ☞ 1625

RESCUE,
Assumption of risks, **Neglig** ☞ 1315
Plaintiff's conduct or fault, **Neglig** ☞ 1293

ROOFS and ceilings,
Breach of duty, **Neglig** ☞ 1116
Construction, demolition and repairs, **Neg-
lig** ☞ 1204(3)

SAFE workplace laws,
Generally, **Neglig** ☞ 1204(5-8)
Frequenter laws, **Neglig** ☞ 1204(8)
Scaffolding laws, **Neglig** ☞ 1204(6)

PREMISES LIABILITY—Cont'd
SAFE workplace laws—Cont'd

Structural work laws, **Neglig** ☞ 1204(7)

SCAFFOLDS. See subheading LADDERS
and scaffolds, under this heading.

SHOWS. See heading **THEATERS AND
SHOWS,** generally.

SIDEWALKS and walkways,
Breach of duty, **Neglig** ☞ 1126
Plaintiff's conduct or fault, **Neglig**
☞ 1291(2)

SLIPS and falls in general,
Breach of duty,
Generally, **Neglig** ☞ 1095
Floors, **Neglig** ☞ 1104(3)
Ice and snow, **Neglig** ☞ 1132
Stairs and ramps, **Neglig** ☞ 1110(1)
Complaint, **Neglig** ☞ 1524(2)
Evidence,
Burden of proof, **Neglig** ☞ 1563
Presumptions and inferences, **Neglig**
☞ 1594
Weight and sufficiency, **Neglig** ☞ 1669
Jury instructions, **Neglig** ☞ 1735
Jury questions and directing verdict, **Neglig**
☞ 1707
Plaintiff's conduct or fault, **Neglig** ☞ 1288

SNOW. See subheading ICE and snow, under
this heading.

SOCIAL guests as licensees, **Neglig**
☞ 1040(4)

SPECTATORS. See heading **THEATERS
AND SHOWS,** generally.

SPORTING events. See heading **THEATERS
AND SHOWS,** generally.

STAIRS and ramps,
Breach of duty,
Generally, **Neglig** ☞ 1110(1-3)
Debris and other objects, **Neglig**
☞ 1110(2)
Hand and guard rails, **Neglig** ☞ 1110(3)
Slips and falls in general, **Neglig**
☞ 1110(1)
Violation of statutory requirements, **Neg-
lig** ☞ 1110(3)
Water and other substances, **Neglig**
☞ 1110(2)

STANDARD of care,
Generally, **Neglig** ☞ 1030-1079
Criminal acts of third persons, **Neglig**
☞ 1070
Due care, **Neglig** ☞ 1032
Firefighters, **Neglig** ☞ 1060

NEGLIGENCE

(C) STANDARD OF CARE.

⚩1031. Not insurer or guarantor.

Tex.App.–Houston [14 Dist.] 2001. Premises owner's duty toward its invitee does not make the possessor an insurer of the invitee's safety.—Wal-Mart Stores, Inc. v. Redding, 56 S.W.3d 141, rehearing overruled.

⚩1037(4). Care required in general.

Ky.App. 2001. Under common law premises liability, the owner of a premises to which the public is invited has a general duty to exercise ordinary care to keep the premises in a reasonably safe condition and warn invitees of dangers that are latent, unknown or not obvious.—Lewis v. B & R Corporation, 56 S.W.3d 432.

Tex.App.–Houston [14 Dist.] 2001. Premises owner's duty toward its invitee does not make the possessor an insurer of the invitee's safety.—Wal-Mart Stores, Inc. v. Redding, 56 S.W.3d 141, rehearing overruled.

⚩1076. —— In general.

Tex.App.–Houston [14 Dist.] 2001. Patron was store's "invitee," and thus store owed her duty to exercise reasonable care to protect her from dangerous conditions in store known or discoverable to it.—Wal-Mart Stores, Inc. v. Redding, 56 S.W.3d 141, rehearing overruled.

(D) BREACH OF DUTY.

⚩1095. Slips and falls in general.

Tex.App.–Houston [14 Dist.] 2001. To recover damages in a slip-and-fall case, a plaintiff must prove: (1) actual or constructive knowledge of some condition on the premises by the owner/operator, (2) that the condition posed an unreasonable risk of harm, (3) that the owner/operator did not exercise reasonable care to reduce or eliminate the risk, and (4) that the owner/operator's failure to use such care proximately caused the plaintiff's injuries.—Wal-Mart Stores, Inc. v. Redding, 56 S.W.3d 141, rehearing overruled.

⚩1101. —— In general.

Ky.App. 2001. Statutes, ordinances, regulations and building codes may create a duty subject to liability as negligence per se.—Lewis v. B & R Corporation, 56 S.W.3d 432.

⚩1104(6). Water and other substances.

Tex.App.–Houston [14 Dist.] 2001. In slip-and-fall cases, the actual or constructive knowledge requirement be met in one of three ways, namely, the invitee may prove: (1) the owner/operator put the foreign substance on the floor, (2) the owner/operator knew that it was on the floor and negligently failed to remove it, or (3) the substance was on the floor so long that, in the exercise of ordinary care, it should have been discovered and removed.—Wal-Mart Stores, Inc. v. Redding, 56 S.W.3d 141, rehearing overruled.

Generally, a plaintiff establishes constructive knowledge of a dangerous condition with evidence that the foreign substance was on the floor so long that it should have been discovered and removed in the exercise of ordinary care.—Id.

XVIII. ACTIONS.

(C) EVIDENCE.

5. WEIGHT AND SUFFICIENCY.

⚩1670. —— Buildings and other structures.

Tex.App.–Houston [14 Dist.] 2001. More than scintilla of evidence existed from which jury could determine that store had actual knowledge of wet mist on floor, which allegedly caused patron to slip and injure herself, for purposes of patron's premises liability action against store, where store patron testified that immediately after she slipped she looked down at floor and noticed it was covered with mist of water, patron immediately told employee, who was standing just beyond area where incident occurred about 15 feet inside entrance, patron testified that employee told patron that she was worried that somebody was going to get hurt because it had been like that all day, and that before accident, floor had been mopped several times.—Wal-Mart Stores, Inc. v. Redding, 56 S.W.3d 141, rehearing overruled.

Evidence was factually sufficient to support jury's implied finding that prior to patron's arrival, store had actual knowledge of dangerous condition created by wet mist on floor where patron slipped, even though manager testified to periodic efforts to ameliorate moisture brought into store by customers, and to warn customers about dangerous condition, which was relevant to issue of whether store exercised reasonable care to reduce or eliminate risk, where patron testified that employee told her she was worried someone might slip, and manager testified that because of weather, store had placed floor mats and caution cones in vestibule area, he did not know if safety cones were out in area where patron slipped, that floor in area where patron slipped had been mopped at various times during day, and mats were not where slip occurred.—Id.

NEGLIGENCE

XVII. PREMISES LIABILITY.

(D) BREACH OF DUTY.

⚷1086. Defect or dangerous conditions generally.

Fla.App. 1 Dist. 2000. Possessor of land cannot refuse to correct a dangerous condition on land for which it is responsible when that danger is expressly called to its attention and then escape all liability as a matter of law when that dangerous condition foreseeably results in injury to another.—Cusick ex rel. Çusick v. City of Neptune Beach, 765 So.2d 175.

⚷1088. —— In general.

Fla.App. 1 Dist. 2000. Possessor of land cannot refuse to correct a dangerous condition on land for which it is responsible when that danger is expressly called to its attention and then escape all liability as a matter of law when that dangerous condition foreseeably results in injury to another.—Cusick ex rel. Cusick v. City of Neptune Beach, 765 So.2d 175.

Fla.App. 4 Dist. 1999. In a slip and fall action, the plaintiff must generally prove that the owner of the premises had actual or constructive knowledge of the causative condition.—Soriano v. B & B Cash Grocery Stores, Inc., 757 So.2d 514, review granted 744 So.2d 456.

⚷1089. —— Constructive notice.

Fla.App. 3 Dist. 2000. Constructive notice of a dangerous condition may be shown by presenting evidence that the condition existed for such a length of time that, in exercise of ordinary care, the defendant should have known of the condition.—Cisneros v. Costco Wholesale Corp., 754 So.2d 819.

⚷1104(4). Inequalities in surface.

Fla.App. 2 Dist. 1998. Customer could not recover from store for injuries sustained in trip and fall allegedly caused by strip of material protruding from area between two floor surfaces, where there was no evidence that store had actual or constructive notice of offending condition, or that floor was improperly installed or maintained.—Fogel v. Staples the Office Superstore, Inc., 750 So.2d 30.

⚷1104(6). Water and other substances.

Fla.App. 5 Dist. 2000. Store patron who slipped and fell on egg on floor was required to prove that store, through its employees, could be charged with constructive knowledge of the dangerous condition, given absence of proof or suggestion that store employee caused egg to fall or that anyone actually saw egg before patron fell.—Hussain v. Winn Dixie Stores, Inc., 765 So.2d 141, rehearing denied.

⚷1104(7). Objects and debris.

Fla.App. 3 Dist. 1999. Nursing home visitor could not prove that nursing home had actual or constructive knowledge of grape on floor and thus nursing home was not liable for visitor's slip and fall on grape; there was no evidence that because three nurses were in vicinity they saw or should have seen grape, there was no evidence to suggest that grape was on floor for a length of time that would place nursing home on reasonable notice of its existence, and there was no evidence of previous instance where food substance was on floor and resulted in injury so as to put nursing home on notice that it should be looking for food.—Markowitz v. Helen Homes of Kendall Corp., 736 So.2d 775, review granted 743 So.2d 509.

⚷1117. —— Elevators and escalators.

Liabilities of owners to passengers, see CARRIERS.

⚷1119. —— Furniture, shelves, displays, carts and other accessories.

Fla.App. 2 Dist. 2000. Store patron established store's liability for injuries sustained when a box containing a van console fell on her head; while walking in a sporting goods aisle, the patron observed two employees transferring merchandise from atop a display to a lower shelf, and as she walked past them, she heard someone say "oh," upon which she turned in the direction of the sound and the employees, was struck on her right forehead, and fell to the floor; as she stood up, she observed a box containing a van console on the ground near where she had fallen.—Wal-Mart Stores, Inc. v. Boertlein, 775 So.2d 345.

⚷1152. —— Adjacent public ways.

Defects in sidewalks or other public ways, see MUNICIPAL CORPORATIONS ⚷808 and HIGHWAYS ⚷199; automobile accidents, see AUTOMOBILES ⚷269, 289.

(G) LIABILITIES RELATING TO CONSTRUCTION, DEMOLITION AND REPAIR.

⚷1204(1). In general.

Fla.App. 3 Dist. 2000. Building owner did not have a duty to warn air conditioning repair person that there were construction items on the second floor where the air conditioning unit was located, where dark lighting conditions were obvious, it was repair person's responsibility to provide the lighting necessary for the work, building appeared to be under construction, and pieces of pipe on which repair person slipped were there to be seen upon any reasonable inspection of the work area.—Roberts v. Dacra Design Associates, Ltd., 766 So.2d 1184.

⚷1205(3). Lenders, financiers and mortgagees.

Non-construction-related liabilities, see ⚷1268.

⚷1205(4). Architects and designers.

Fla.App. 4 Dist. 2000. Allegations that architect prepared erroneous design documents with knowledge that owner would supply them to the successful bidder, and that successful bidder would be injured if they were inadequate, were sufficient to establish a special relationship between architect and general contractor that was the successful bidder, supporting general contractor's action for professional malpractice against architect despite lack of contract between general contractor and architect.—Hewett-Kier Const., Inc. v. Lemuel Ramos and Associates, Inc., 775 So.2d 373, rehearing denied.

⚷1205(5). Engineers.

Fla. 1999. Homeowner could bring negligence claim against engineers who allegedly failed to detect and disclose certain defects in condition of home inspected, although neither engineer signed contract between homeowner and engineering firm, their employer, where engineers were designated by employer to perform engineering services for homeowner, and both were responsible for performing professional services to a client of their company whom they reasonably knew or should have known would be injured if they were negligent in the performance of those services. West's F.S.A. §§ 471.023, 621.07.—Moransais v. Heathman, 744 So.2d 973, rehearing denied.

⚷1205(7). —— In general.

Fla.App. 4 Dist. 1997. Contractors may share responsibility for injuries caused on or around construction site even though landowner retains some possession and control of premises.—Worth v. Eugene Gentile Builders, 744 So.2d 1014, opin-

Patricia MARKOWITZ and Robert Markowitz, Appellants,

v.

HELEN HOMES OF KENDALL CORPORATION, a/k/a Kendall Health Care Properties, d/b/a The Palace Living Facility, Appellee.

No. 98–452.

District Court of Appeal of Florida, Third District.

July 7, 1999.

Visitor brought slip and fall action against nursing home. The Circuit Court, Dade County, Thomas S. Wilson Jr., J., granted summary judgment to nursing home. Visitor appealed. The District Court of Appeal held that visitor could not prove that nursing home had actual or constructive knowledge of grape on floor.

Affirmed.

Negligence ⚷1104(7)

Nursing home visitor could not prove that nursing home had actual or constructive knowledge of grape on floor and thus nursing home was not liable for visitor's slip and fall on grape; there was no evidence that because three nurses were in vicinity they saw or should have seen grape, there was no evidence to suggest that grape was on floor for a length of time that would place nursing home on reasonable notice of its existence, and there was no evidence of previous instance where food substance was on floor and resulted in injury so as to put nursing home on notice that it should be looking for food.

Podhurst, Orseck, Josefsberg, Eaton, Meadow, Olin & Perwin and Joel D. Eaton, Miami, for appellant.

Kubicki Draper and Angela C. Flowers, Ft. Lauderdale, for appellee.

Before JORGENSON, COPE, and LEVY, JJ.

PER CURIAM.

This is an appeal from a trial court Order granting defendant/Helen Homes of Kendall Corporation's ("the nursing home") Motion for Summary Judgment and denying the plaintiffs/Patricia and Robert Markowitz's ("the Markowitzes") Motion for Summary Judgment. We affirm.

The Markowitzes brought suit against the nursing home alleging that Mrs. Markowitz slipped and fell on a grape in the main area of the nursing home facility and sustained serious injuries while visiting her mother, a resident at the nursing home. The Complaint alleges that the nursing home knew or should have known of the dangerous condition but negligently failed to correct it.

After discovery, the nursing home moved for summary judgment contending that there was no evidence that the defendant had actual knowledge of the presence of the grape, or that the grape was on the floor for a sufficient length of time to provide it with constructive notice of its presence. The Markowitzes responded that three of the nursing home's employees were engaged in a conversation in the immediate vicinity of the fall and should have been aware of the presence of the grape. Additionally, the Markowitzes attached the affidavit of an expert nursing home administrator who stated that permitting elderly residents to carry food from the dining room to their room was unreasonably dangerous. The nursing home relied on the testimony of the nurses, who denied knowledge of the presence of the grape, and the deposition of the building supervisor and the housekeeper, who each testified that the nursing home's policy was that common areas are swept and cleaned several times throughout the day. The trial court granted the nursing home's motion and entered Final Summary Judgment.

We affirm the entry of Final Summary Judgment because the Markowitzes are unable to prove that the nursing home had actual or constructive knowledge of the spilt grape. *See Miller v. Big C Trading, Inc.*, 641 So.2d 911 (Fla. 3d DCA 1994); *see also Publix Super Market, Inc. v. Sanchez*, 700 So.2d 405 (Fla. 3d DCA 1997). There is no evidence in the record to support the Markowitzes' contention that because three nurses were in the vicinity of the fall they saw or should have seen the grape. Furthermore, there is no evidence to suggest that the grape was on the floor for a length of time that would place the nursing home on reasonable notice of its existence. Additionally, the Markowitzes are unable to establish that the nursing home's method of operation is negligent. *Publix Super Market, Inc. v. Sanchez*, 700 So.2d at 406. There is no evidence of a previous instance where a grape or other food substance was on the floor and resulted in injury to a resident or visitor so as to put the nursing home on notice that they should be looking for food.

Affirmed.

Tessie SCHUSSEL, Appellant/Cross–Appellee,

v.

LADD HAIRDRESSERS, INC., d/b/a Hair & Company, a Florida corporation, Appellee/Cross–Appellant.

Nos. 98–1713, 98–1853.

District Court of Appeal of Florida, Fourth District.

July 7, 1999.

Patron brought trip and fall action against owner of hairdressing shop. The Circuit Court, Broward County, John T. Luzzo, J., entered judgment on jury verdict for shop owner and denied shop owner's motion to tax costs and attorney's fees. Shop owner appealed. The District Court of Appeal, Hazouri, J., held that shop owner's offer of judgment was untimely and unenforceable because it was made less than 45 days before the first day of the docket on which the case was set for trial.

Affirmed.

1. Costs ⚿42(4)

Defendant's offer of judgment was untimely and thus unenforceable because it was made less than 45 days before the first day of the docket on which the case was set for trial, even though case actually went to trial almost six months after it was first set for trial, after defendant was granted a continuance over plaintiff's objection. West's F.S.A. RCP Rule 1.442(b).

2. Costs ⚿42(2)

Statute governing offers of judgment and rule of civil procedure governing proposals for settlement must be strictly construed, as they are punitive in nature in that they impose sanctions upon the losing party and are in derogation of the common law. West's F.S.A. § 768.79; West's F.S.A. RCP Rule 1.442.

Pamela Beckham of Beckham & Beckham, P.A., North Miami Beach, for appellant/cross-appellee.

Hinda Klein of Conroy, Simberg & Ganon, P.A., Hollywood, for appellee/cross-appellant.

HAZOURI, J.

This is an appeal by the plaintiff, Tessie Schussel (Schussel), of a final judgment for the defendant, Ladd Hairdressers, Inc. (Ladd), entered pursuant to a jury's ver-

789So2d[1]1186
d 790So2d513
791So2d1128
791So2d1228
d 26FLW(D) [1623
26FLW(D) [2016
26FLW(D) [2453

—89—
s 2001FlaApp [LX12751

—91—
q 2001FL LX [610
q 26FLW(S)174

—93—
773So2d623

—94—
Autrey v State
f 789So2d[1]1148

—96—
2001FlaApp [LX16037

—97—
2001FlaApp [LX[3]7933
2001FlaApp [LX9183
f 2001FlaApp [LX[4]9826
773So2d1238
790So2d1140
f 790So2d[4]1177
791So2d[3]44
26FLW(D)[3] [1458
26FLW(D) [1657
f 26FLW(D)[4] [1728

—103—
j 2001FlaApp [LX13465
j 26FLW(D) [2350

—106—
De 2000FL LX [556
De 760So2d947
2001WLR29

—111—
Gr 2000FL LX [491
Gr 761So2d330
a 780So2d6
768So2d1067

—118—
772So2d564

—119—
774So2d806
o 789So2d402
789So2d[1]402

—124—
s 777So2d1185
2001FlaApp [LX11076
26FLW(D) [1917

—130—
s 783So2d1208

—133—
2001FlaApp [LX[2]12897
2001FlaApp [LX[1]12897
793So2d[1]1165
793So2d[2]1165
26FLW(D)[1] [2237
26FLW(D)[2] [2237

—134—
771So2d1253

—138—
771So2d569

—157—
Royal v State
2000FlaApp [LX9758
764So2d597
772So2d50
778So2d537

—698—
775So2d1017
787So2d[1]149

—699—
f 2001FlaApp [LX10635
d 788So2d1082
f 791So2d544
f 26FLW(D) [1848

—705—
2001FlaApp [LX[2]12260
792So2d[2]708
26FLW(D)[2] [2129

—708—
789So2d985

—713—
773So2d80
787So2d932

—719—
f 2001FlaApp [LX9199
770So2d297
f 26FLW(D) [1666

—722—
f 2001FlaApp [LX6689
2001FlaApp [LX7475
2001FlaApp [LX[1]13019
779So2d412
779So2d534
f 26FLW(D) [1234
26FLW(D) [1380
26FLW(D)[1] [2223

—724—
2001FlaApp [LX[3]7459
783So2d1119
787So2d197
791So2d[3]38
26FLW(D)[3] [1378

—726—
2000FlaApp [LX[1]12577
780So2d[1]152
780So2d[2]152
780So2d[3]152
786So2d1222
787So2d227
25FLW(D)[1] [2345

—728—
s 774So2d26
~ 779So2d521

—732—
~ 2001FlaApp [LX[7]13434
787So2d930
~ 26FLW(D)[7] [2437

—734—
Katz v State
cc 771So2d1248

—735—
780So2d192

—736—
786So2d29
787So2d835

—741—
d 2001FlaApp [LX8774
j 2001FlaApp [LX8774
d 791So2d491
j 791So2d491
d 26FLW(D) [1595
j 26FLW(D) [1595

—745—
De 2000FL LX [765
De 762So2d917
2001FlaApp [LX12482
776So2d1018
783So2d1163
795So2d169
26FLW(D) [2151

—757—
2001FlaApp [LX4195
2001FlaApp [LX14480
785So2d500
26FLW(D) [2483

—761—
c 2001FlaApp [LX[1]9498
c 786So2d647
c 790So2d[1]1151
c 26FLW(D)[1] [1681

—775—
788So2d286

—776—
2000FlaApp [LX[2]6218
j 2000FlaApp [LX6218
d 2001FlaApp [LX13794
2001FlaApp [LX[1]14877
~ 2001FlaApp [LX15748
e 768So2d526
784So2d[2]1197
788So2d[2]265
j 788So2d270
j 25FLW(D) [1259
25FLW(D)[2] [1259
d 26FLW(D) [2356
26FLW(D)[1] [2526

—780—
2001FlaApp [LX14704
778So2d[3]1053
789So2d[2]1231
26FLW(D) [2502

—782—
Gr 2000FL LX [535
Gr 761So2d328
776So2d323

—786—
cc 2001FlaApp [LX11262

—794—
2001FlaApp [LX7155
2001FlaApp [LX[1]12480
2001FlaApp [LX13842
j 782So2d899
785So2d517
790So2d466
26FLW(D) [1302
26FLW(D)[1] [2144
26FLW(D) [2357

—796—
j 2000FlaApp [LX6218
f 2001FlaApp [LX13794
2001FlaApp [LX16263
771So2d46
~ 771So2d46
c 787So2d175
j 788So2d269
j 25FLW(D) [1259
f 26FLW(D) [2356

—798—
2000FlaApp [LX11640
779So2d[1]456
25FLW(D) [2209

—803—
773So2d[3]1280

—807—
Baker v State
s 776So2d374
s 789So2d549

—811—
779So2d587

—1150—
776So2d979
j 776So2d983

—1151—
Blish v Atlanta Cas. Co.
2001FL LX [2265

—1160—
2001FlaApp [LX[6]11124
780So2d279
792So2d[6]583
26FLW(D)[6] [1914
52FLR1039

—1167—
2001FlaApp [LX11251
773So2d1193
791So2d581
26FLW(D) [1936

—1211—
j 2001FlaApp [LX8774
j 791So2d491
j 26FLW(D) [1595

—1217—
f 789So2d1018
789So2d[2]1018

—1221—
f 2001FlaApp [LX[1]13457
f 26FLW(D)[1] [2340

—1222—
De 2000FL LX [329
De 751So2d [1251

—1224—
771So2d1254

—1231—
~ 2001FlaApp [LX3353
2001FlaApp [LX7473
q 2001FlaApp [LX15677
2001FL LX610
j 2001FL LX [610
772So2d36
779So2d516
780So2d[1]978
783So2d371
26FLW(S)174
j 26FLW(S)174
~ 26FLW(D) [759
26FLW(D) [1379

—1241—
US cert den
528US1123

—1242—
2000FlaApp [LX16978
775So2d304

—1248—
2000FlaApp [LX17889
781So2d1091

—1251—
2001FlaApp [LX14896
777So2d[2]1085
777So2d[3]1085
26FLW(D) [2532

—1256—
Hope v State
r 2001FL LX [1928
r 26FLW(S)651

Index

C

D

E

F

G

H

I

S

T

U

V

W

WEST HILLS COLLEGE